A CRITICAL EXAMINATION
OF THE ORIENTATION POSTULATE
IN ACCOUNTING
WITH PARTICULAR ATTENTION TO
ITS HISTORICAL DEVELOPMENT

This is a volume in the Arno Press collection

THE DEVELOPMENT
OF CONTEMPORARY
ACCOUNTING THOUGHT

Advisory Editor
Richard P. Brief

Editorial Board
Gary John Previts
Basil S. Yamey
Stephen A. Zeff

*See last pages of this volume
for a complete list of titles.*

A CRITICAL EXAMINATION
OF THE ORIENTATION POSTULATE
IN ACCOUNTING
WITH PARTICULAR ATTENTION TO
ITS HISTORICAL DEVELOPMENT

Stephen Addam Zeff

ARNO PRESS
A New York Times Company
New York • 1978

**Publisher's Note: This book has been reproduced
from the best available copy.**

Editorial Supervision: LUCILLE MAIORCA

———◆———

First publication 1978 by Arno Press Inc.

Copyright © 1978 by Stephen Addam Zeff

THE DEVELOPMENT OF CONTEMPORARY ACCOUNTING THOUGHT
ISBN for complete set: 0-405-10891-5
See last pages of this volume for titles.

Manufactured in the United States of America

———◆———

Library of Congress Cataloging in Publication Data

Zeff, Stephen A.
    A critical examination of the orientation postulate
in accounting with particular attention to its
historical development.

    (The Development of contemporary accounting thought)
    Originally presented as the author's thesis,
University of Michigan, 1961.
    Bibliography: p.
    1. Accounting--History. I. Title. II. Series.
HF5625.Z43 1978   657'.09   77-87306
ISBN 0-405-10945-8

A CRITICAL EXAMINATION OF THE ORIENTATION POSTULATE IN

ACCOUNTING, WITH PARTICULAR ATTENTION TO

ITS HISTORICAL DEVELOPMENT

by
Stephen Addam Zeff

A dissertation submitted in partial fulfillment
of the requirements for the degree of
Doctor of Philosophy in the
University of Michigan
1961

Doctoral Committee:

      Professor William J. Schlatter, Chairman
      Professor Herbert E. Miller
      Professor Wilford J. Eiteman
      Associate Professor James C. T. Mao
      Professor Alan N. Polasky

PREFACE

This writer wishes to acknowledge the helpful advice and encouragement throughout the preparation of this dissertation of Professors William J. Schlatter and Herbert E. Miller. A large intellectual debt is owed to Professor Emeritus William A. Paton, whose incisive analysis and rigorously logical theory of accounts first stimulated this writer to think critically about accounting problems. The views expressed in this study are, of course, those of the author, and not necessarily those of the aforementioned persons.

Appreciation is also due to the United States Steel Foundation, which, via a generous grant, contributed significantly to the comparative dispatch with which this study has been completed. A formal proposal was submitted to the Graduate Studies Committee of the School of Business Administration on September 30, 1960; the final draft prior to inspection by the dissertation committee was completed in mid-May, 1961.

A doctoral dissertation should serve two purposes. First, it should encourage the candidate to inquire intensively into a limited subject area in order to add substantially to his knowledge, and, it is to be hoped, to that of others, about matters that were previously surrounded by unanswered questions. Second, its completion should encourage

the candidate who aspires to a mastery of his discipline to
pursue the solutions of more complex enigmas as a part of
the unending efforts of scholars to seek out and disseminate
the truth. No small portion of the candidate's future endeavors, therefore, should involve classroom teaching, individual counseling, speaking, and publishing--activities that
are intended to assist students in (1) adding to their knowledge and (2) developing a scholarly attitude toward the solution of new and challenging problems.

It is in the spirit of this philosophy that this
project has been conceived and executed.

Accordingly, this work is dedicated TO MY STUDENTS.

TABLE OF CONTENTS

LIST OF ILLUSTRATIONS

CHAPTER I

NATURE OF THE PROBLEM, AND OBJECTIVES

Inherent in the theoretical schema of accounting writers is a perspective from which the accounting process is to be viewed. Some writers make explicit their choice of a perspective, occasionally giving reasons therefor; other writers leave the matter unsaid. But a perspective must find expression somewhere in the theoretical construct, for accounting must relate to one or more persons, organizations, or activities.

As will become abundantly evident, accounting writers evince a large measure of disagreement not only over the perspective that is most suitable in a given set of circumstances but also over the range of choices that are available. It is not even clear that accountants agree upon the criteria to be employed in choosing a perspective.

Evidence of the Disharmony

An inspection of accounting literature discloses that writers usually depict those who disagree on a perspective, or viewpoint, as coming from two opposing garrisons: that which defends the "proprietary theory" and that which guards the "entity theory." Until Chapter IV, it will suffice to define the "proprietary theory" as calling for central accounting attention to be directed at the proprietor, the accounting being made for his financial interest in the firm. The "entity theory," on the other hand, implies that the enterprise is the appropriate accounting setting, the proprietor being one of the several financially interested parties therein. Both "theories" presume that separate records are kept for business and (the owner's) household affairs.

Newlove and Garner, whose discussion will be reintroduced in Chapter IV, caution accountants who would view the matter of a perspective too lightly:

> The two theories . . . do not offer a common meeting ground, and if an accountant is not persistent in holding to one or the other, his conclusions as to matters of interest are likely to be inconsistent and unreconcilable. In addition, if one person holds to the entity theory, for example, in deciding the proper attitude to take on a certain question, and a second person adopts the proprietary theory in making his decision on the same point, the two may argue and discuss for days without reaching a common decision. In a sense, they are simply not using the same language. Their assumptions being different, their viewpoints may be irreconcilable.[1]
>
> . . . .
>
> Much damage has been done by the conscious or unconscious shifting of viewpoints (or theories), and a 'clearing of the atmosphere' would result if one or the other of the theories were adopted in toto.[2]

And again:

> Differences [between the two theories and their implications for the remainder of accounting theory] are real and not just superficial; they strike at the very nature of the accounting process.[3]

---

[1] George Hillis Newlove and S. Paul Garner, Advanced Accounting, Vol. I: Corporate Capital and Income (2 vols.; Boston: D. C. Heath and Company, 1951), 20; footnote omitted.

[2] Ibid., I, 23. [3] Ibid., I, 22.

That the amount of influence which the law should have on
accounting theory and practice remains a question still subject to much debate, assert the authors, has not aided in
the resolution of the discord over an accounting viewpoint.[1]

Gilman, in a somewhat more compromising tone, writes:

> Both the entity and proprietary conventions have
> value. Like all conventions, each contains an ele-
> ment of artificiality. Either is valuable so long
> as it is consistently maintained. It is only when
> an unconscious shift in viewpoint from one to the
> other occurs that there is danger of false reason-
> ing.[2]

Yet accounting writers allude to a schism that divides
such respected accounting theorists as Sprague, Hatfield,
Kester, Paton, and Littleton. The former three, according
to Gilman[3] and Paton,[4] advocate the "proprietary theory."
Paton and Littleton,[5] however, are arrayed on the side of
the "entity theory." To be sure, many other accounting wri-

---

[1]Ibid., I, 23.

[2]Stephen Gilman, Accounting Concepts of Profit
(New York: The Ronald Press Company, 1939), p. 50.

[3]Ibid.

[4]William Andrew Paton, Accounting Theory--With
Special Reference to the Corporate Enterprise (New York: The
Ronald Press Company, 1922), pp. 111, 51-52. Also see A. C.
Littleton, Accounting Evolution to 1900 (New York: American
Institute Publishing Co., Inc., 1933), p. 184.

[5]Their joint effort is W. A. Paton and A. C. Little-
ton, An Introduction to Corporate Accounting Standards
(Chicago: American Accounting Association, 1940), Monograph
No. 3. They are described as advocating the "entity theory"
by George R. Husband, "The Entity Concept in Accounting,"
The Accounting Review, XXIX, No. 4 (October, 1954), 552-63.

4

ters have joined the dispute. Gilman believes that the
"entity theory" is implicit in the use of double-entry bookkeeping.[1] But no less an authority than Vatter rejects both
theories.[2] Still another writer urges that the large corporation be viewed in its relation to society.[3] These and
other views will be reviewed at length in Chapter V.

But how profound are these differences of opinion?
Newlove and Garner detail 14 ways in which the two theories
disagree.[4] Some of them are: nature of profits, nature of
capital, primary purpose of accounting, nature of assets,
importance of periodicity to profits, and relation of expenses to assets. As the authors state, "Even a casual investigation reveals that the [14] distinctions . . . strike at the
very heart of the accounting process."[5]

One writer even states that the "proprietary theory"
implies the use of periodic market-value revisions of the
owner's investment as the means of determining "profit."[6]
Here there would be no "matching process" in the conventional

[1]Gilman, op. cit., pp. 52-53.

[2]William J. Vatter, The Fund Theory of Accounting and
Its Implications for Financial Reports (Chicago: The University of Chicago Press, 1947), p. 7.

[3]Waino W. Suojanen, "Accounting Theory and the Large
Corporation," The Accounting Review, XXIX, No. 3 (July, 1954),
391-98.

[4]Newlove and Garner, op. cit., I, 21-22.

[5]Ibid., I, 25.

[6]Vatter, op. cit., p. 4.

sense.[1]

Notwithstanding the alleged gulf between the two
major theories, other writings tend to suggest that the magnitude of the difference is much less--and that the choice
depends largely on the legal nature of the form of business
organization for which the accounting is commissioned.[2]

It can be shown, therefore, that (1) at least two
opposing theories have been advanced, (2) renowned accounting theorists are said to support each view (as well as
other views), and (3) the size and accounting significance
of the gap between the "proprietary theory" and "entity
theory" are represented as being substantial, although full
agreement on this point is lacking. Furthermore, it can be
demonstrated that the nature of the implications of each
major viewpoint for accounting theory is not at all clear,
the literature containing contradictory and inconsistent
opinions in this regard.

For example, Husband contends that the "entity theory"
inexorably requires that a stock dividend be treated as in-

---

[1]For a discussion of the conventional "matching process," consult Paton and Littleton, op. cit., especially pp.
14-18, 69-72. In short, the "matching process" involves the
relating to revenues of causally-associated expirations of
asset values in order to ascertain the resulting net income.

[2]See, for example, the suggested answers to Question
No. 8 of the "Theory of Accounts" phase of the Uniform C. P. A.
Examination, May 13-15, 1959: "Professional Examinations,"
The Accounting Review, XXXIV, No. 4 (October, 1959), 684-85;
and "Accounting Education," The Journal of Accountancy, CVIII,
No. 4 (October, 1959), 67-68.

come to the stockholders.[1] For this and other reasons, Husband adopts another perspective (very similar to the "proprietary theory") that, according to Husband, allows the interpretation of a stock dividend as nothing more than a proliferation of the number of shares. Yet Paton, who professes the "entity theory," steadfastly denies that a stock dividend produces income for the stockholders.[2] Indeed, he claims that the perspective that Husband prefers "underlies, at least implicitly, the persisting minority view that somehow 'dividend' shares represent income to the stockholders."[3]

As another example, the authors of two recent introductory accounting textbooks take the position that the accounting unit should be the business enterprise, not the collective owners.[4] But one of these texts defines "net income" (or "income") as the return to all suppliers of long-term capital,[5] while the other defines it as the return to the

---

[1]George R. Husband, "The Corporate-Entity Fiction and Accounting Theory," The Accounting Review, XIII, No. 3 (September, 1938), 246-48.

[2]William A. Paton and William A. Paton, Jr., Corporation Accounts and Statements (New York: The Macmillan Company, 1955), pp. 122-31.

[3]Ibid., p. 3.

[4]Perry Mason, Sidney Davidson, and James S. Schindler, Fundamentals of Accounting (4th ed.; New York: Henry Holt and Company, Inc., 1959); and Homer A. Black and John E. Champion, Accounting in Business Decisions: Theory, Method, and Use (Englewood Cliffs, N. J.: Prentice-Hall, Inc., 1961). It is interesting to note that all five authors are former students of W. A. Paton.

[5]Mason, Davidson, and Schindler, ibid., pp. 19, 281.

residual equity holders.[1] Moonitz and Staehling also declare
for the "entity theory," but later state that "the primary
purpose or objective [of accounting] is the recording of
changes in net worth or proprietorship. . . ."[2] The Newlove-
Garner conception of "income"--in accord with the "entity
theory"--is that of a return to the residual equity.[3] But
Paton's "entity theory" reflects "income" as the return to
all long-term capital suppliers.[4] Are these two interpretations of the "entity theory" mutually consistent?

Finally, although no citations will be offered at
this point, it can be shown that there is substantial disagreement, already suggested by Newlove and Garner, over the
criteria that should be used in selecting an accounting perspective. At one extreme, some writers would consider only
legal phenomena as controlling. At the other, solely economic factors are deemed as relevant. Most writers seem to
use some of each.

An "overhaul" of these diverse and often conflicting
views and implications thereof is clearly needed. The maze
of perspectives demands a re-ordering and re-evaluation. The
accounting perspective--also referred to in this study as the

---

[1]Black and Champion, op. cit., pp. 11-12, chap. 3.

[2]Maurice Moonitz and Charles C. Staehling, Accounting: An Analysis of Its Problems (2 vols.; Brooklyn: The
Foundation Press, Inc., 1952), I, 4-5, 18.

[3]Newlove and Garner, op. cit., I, 21, item 8.

[4]Paton and Paton, op. cit., pp. 275-77.

"orientation postulate"[1]--requires a substantial amount of clarification. If Littleton is correct in describing the determination of "income" as the most important accounting task,[2] a question that impinges on the nature of "income" as greatly as does that which surrounds the orientation postulate possesses a very large measure of significance to accountants.

Objectives of the Study

It is therefore the multipartite purpose of this study to (1) survey the choices that are available, (2) discuss the factors that are relevant in choosing a point of view, (3) assay the relative merits of each possibility, and (4) propose in general terms a desirable perspective--or perspectives, if more than one is both desirable and feasible--that best effectuates the accounting process.

A great deal has been written on this question, but no attempt has yet been offered at interrelating in a logical manner the multifarious perspectives that have been urged by accountants, and only a few efforts exist at trying to explain the reasons for the presence of such diverse views. An historical discussion of the progression of ideas from the more imperfectly communicated notions of the Middle Ages to

---

[1]The reason for choosing the term "postulate" rather than "theory" or "concept" will be disclosed in Chapter III.

[2]A. C. Littleton, Structure of Accounting Theory (Urbana, Ill.: American Accounting Association, 1953), Monograph No. 5, chap. 2.

the most recent articulations of a viewpoint in the mid-
twentieth century will place the entire question of the
accounting perspective in a manageable focus. But the study
will not be solely a chronology of developments. The merits
and limitations of each perspective will be noted and anal-
yzed--whether the authors of the viewpoints have done so or
not. Some that would seem to have validity today may be rejected; some that are viewed as having lost their usefulness
some time ago may be revived for application today.

The study will deal exclusively with that part of
the accounting process that leads to the preparation of periodic financial statements--that is, so-called "financial
accounting."

Outline of the Chapters

The manner of the subsequent development of this
study is as follows: Chapter II attempts to trace the roughly
parallel evolution of accounting and capitalism in order to
demonstrate the importance of the former to the latter, and
vice versa. This historical survey will be useful in ex-
plaining the causes--rooted to a significant extent in changing economic institutions and market structures--of fundamental changes in the accounting process, with particular
reference to their impact on the orientation postulate.

Chapter III reviews the development up to the beginning of the twentieth century of the accounting process, especially as such development has affected the accounting
perspective.

In Chapter IV, the writings--relative to the orientation postulate--of the major accounting theorists of the early twentieth century are given critical examination. A theoretical framework, including a suggested terminology, is proposed in order to sharpen the distinctions between the numerous viewpoints. Also, the basic characteristics of the "proprietary theory" and "entity theory" are explored and criticized.

Chapter V contains a critical review of recent commentary on the older viewpoints as well as of newly discovered perspectives. Special attention is directed to the interpretation of income taxes in the "entity-theory" income statement.

Chapter VI consists of an endeavor to reconcile further some of the conflicting ideas in an effort to present a tentative answer to the question of "What should be the 'orientation postulate'?"

The conclusions and recommendations contained in this study are intended to be the basis of a more effective inquiry by accounting writers into the logical underpinnings of accounting theory. The subject of this study is admittedly quite controversial, and the opinions of this writer--as expressed below--are offered in the expectation that they will generate further critical investigation and, finally, it is hoped, a clarification of issues involved.

CHAPTER II

THE INTERDEPENDENCE OF BOOKKEEPING AND

CAPITALISM: AN HISTORICAL PERSPECTIVE

"The significance of systematic bookkeeping for the development of capitalism . . . can hardly be exaggerated,"[1] writes economic historian Frederick L. Nussbaum. "One cannot imagine," observes German economic historian Werner Sombart, "what capitalism would be without double-entry bookkeeping: the two phenomena are connected as intimately as form and contents."[2] Moreover, it is Schumpeter who writes that "capitalist practice turns the unit of money into a tool of rational cost-profit calculations, of which the towering monument is double-entry bookkeeping."[3]

Such enthusiastic endorsement of the accountant's wares underscores his importance to the profit-maximizing

---

[1]Frederick L. Nussbaum, A History of the Economic Institutions of Modern Europe (New York: F. S. Crofts & Co., 1933), p. 159. This volume is intended to be an introduction to Der Moderne Kapitalismus, by Werner Sombart.

[2]Werner Sombart, "Medieval and Modern Commercial Enterprise," in Frederic C. Lane and Jelle C. Riemersma (editors), Enterprise and Secular Change (Homewood, Ill.: Richard D. Irwin, Inc., 1953), p. 38.

[3]Joseph A. Schumpeter, Capitalism, Socialism, and Democracy (3rd ed.; New York: Harper & Brothers, 1950), p. 123.

function. Furthermore, it militates against any study of
the historical development of accounting which would ignore
the corresponding development of capitalism. Accounting, as
a means of financial communication, should not be examined
in a vacuum.

Accounting reports are desired not because they are
aesthetically beautiful or sensuously pleasing, but because
they contain insights which are of assistance in understand-
ing economic phenomena. Their value resides in their usefulness. And their usefulness stems from a capacity to enable others to pierce the complexities of modern business
enterprise. Thus, as the business enterprise has developed,
so would one expect its system of financial communication to
develop.

It is the task of this chapter to trace, up to the
last decades of the nineteenth century, the broad outlines
of capitalistic development in juxtaposition with the progress of systematic bookkeeping. The changing forms of business enterprise will also, of necessity, be noted. With
this partly-descriptive, partly-analytical preface providing
the necessary historical perspective, the ensuing discussion
of certain aspects of the twentieth-century development of
accounting thought will not seem as if it were emerging from
an eventless past. For it is this writer's thesis that the
accountant's view of a business venture, to be at all useful,
must be shaped by the surrounding economic realities of the
day. As these realities change, the accountant must recon-

sider his point of view. This study, as already noted, seeks to survey the alternative "views" and recommend changes where necessary.

Introductory Notes

Although an early accounting historian writes that "the history of accountancy is, in a large measure, the history of civilization,"[1] this chapter is concerned mainly with the last 750 years. Few would deny that among the requisites of trade, however primitive, are determinations of good and bad, desirable and undesirable, gain and loss. These kinds of calculations are essential per se to barter and other forms of exchange.

An interesting entity-like relationship is said to have existed in the later years of the Roman Empire.[2] Wealthy Romans, believing it beneath their dignity to enter into commercial dealings, delegated the handling of their gainful activities to educated slaves. A kind of "agency bookkeeping" resulted, whereby the slave's records reflected money received from his master as a loan. What might be viewed by some as an ordinary proprietor-proprietorship operation in reality was treated as principal-agent. Indeed, the agent regarded himself as a distinct entity, though sub-

---

[1]Arthur H. Woolf, A Short History of Accountants and Accountancy (London: Gee & Co., 1912), p. xix.

[2]A. C. Littleton, Accounting Evolution to 1900 (New York: American Institute Publishing Co., Inc., 1933), pp. 29-34; and Stephen Gilman, Accounting Concepts of Profit (New York: The Ronald Press Company, 1939), chap. 4.

ject in every respect to the wishes of his master. Gilman,
who sees in this early example of entity-like bookkeeping
the germ of modern accounting theory,[1] interprets the Romans'
principal-agent conception as quite rational. "Because the
slave was a human being with a personality and a viewpoint
of his own," he reasons, "it was natural for the slave to
adopt the record keeping viewpoint that he personally owed
that amount to his master."[2] The slave was not merely the
locus and personification of the master's business dealings;
he saw himself as a separate economic being.

     But Roman bookkeeping went the way of the Roman
Empire. After the death of Theodosius the Great in 395 A.D.
and the resultant confusion of the fifth and sixth centuries,
formal bookkeeping was almost nonexistent until the eleventh
century.[3] And, as will be seen, the Roman patrician was re-
placed by the merchant, and his slave by an impersonal trading firm. Lacking the slave's human qualities, the firm came
to be viewed as an economic offspring (which it was) of the
merchant. One might speculate whether the agency concept
might have been carried forward to the merchant's time, had
the centuries-long quietude of the so-called Dark Ages not
followed in its wake. As it happened, however, the merchant
was depicted as the owner, not the creditor, of his firm.

---

[1] Gilman, ibid., p. 45.

[2] Ibid., p. 39.

[3] Kenneth MacNeal, Truth in Accounting (Philadelphia:
University of Pennsylvania Press, 1939), p. 58.

More relevant to this investigation, however, is the evolution of systematic bookkeeping which paralleled the emergence of capitalism.

Petty Capitalism--Stage For Single-Entry Bookkeeping

If the objective of economic activity under capitalism is "acquisition," as Sombart contends,[1] then the early beginnings of Western capitalism can be traced to the thirteenth century.

Gras delineates three stages in the development of Western capitalism: pre-business capitalism, private-business capitalism, and public-business capitalism.[2] The "pre-business" variety encompasses the pastoral, primitive state, where regular exchange is largely absent. Public-business capitalism is "complete socialism or communism."[3] Clearly, our concern is with the second stage.

Private-business capitalism may be subdivided into petty capitalism, mercantile (commercial) capitalism, industrial capitalism, and financial capitalism.[4]

---

[1] Werner Sombart, "Capitalism," in Edwin R. A. Seligman and Alvin Johnson (editors), Encyclopaedia of the Social Sciences (15 vols.; New York: The Macmillan Company, 1930-35), III, 196.

[2] N. S. B. Gras, "Capitalism--Concepts and History," in Lane and Riemersma, op. cit., pp. 70-71.

[3] Ibid.

[4] "Financial capitalism," according to Gras, was the reign of Wall Street and the investment bankers; the period begins during the closing years of the nineteenth century and concludes with the Great Depression. Because of its histor-

Traveling merchants, small shopkeepers, hucksters, and peddlers characterized petty capitalism. Barter was the chief mode of exchange. The typical merchant was a craftsman or specialist. According to Sombart, the "petty capitalist" was possessed of an "artisanlike mentality."[1]

Honesty and faithfulness to contract were distinctive virtues of the day; furthermore, it was believed that a person should earn only what is necessary to his subsistence, that is, "appropriate to one's station." Strong ethical and religious tenets held that each should seek only a "Christian profit." Indeed, profits were often thought to be the blessing of God on the devout. Advertising, it follows, was regarded as "mean and shameful."[2] Retirement at an early age was common, many merchants buying seats in Parliament for later-life amusement. Such was the economic hollowness--by present-day standards--of petty capitalism.

It would come as no surprise, therefore, that the bookkeeping of the day was limited to keeping track of debts. No record was even kept, as a rule, of cash or barter transactions. Gras calls this crude record-keeping "adequate for their needs [although] there was no means of maintaining ade-

ical location, and because this chapter is concerned with events leading up to the close of the nineteenth century, treatment of "financial capitalism" is omitted from the chapter. Ibid., pp. 77-78, and N. S. B. Gras, Business and Capitalism: An Introduction to Business History (New York: F. S. Crofts & Co., 1939), chap. 6.

[1]Sombart in Lane and Riemersma, op. cit., p. 27.

[2]Nussbaum, op. cit., pp. 153-55.

quate records of the business should it become large or com-
plicated."[1]

Mercantile Capitalism--The Coming Of Double-Entry

The early evolution of capitalism and of systematic
bookkeeping was confined almost solely to Italy. During the
early Middle Ages, the city-states of Northern Italy almost
alone in Europe had retained some of the culture and enterprise of the Roman Empire. They preserved the precepts of
Roman law and were able to remain mostly apart from the feudal
system. Even though among their citizens the ability to per-
form long division was regarded as a mark of high learning,
the standard of literacy was higher than that of anywhere
else in Europe. Due to the Crusades of the eleventh through
thirteenth centuries, the Italian commercial position was
strong. The geographical location of Venice and Genoa especially, was instrumental in establishing Italy as an important intermediary in the burgeoning Oriental trade.[2]
Italy was consequently poised in the thirteenth century to
lead the rest of Europe in early capitalistic achievements.

Petty capitalism remained dominant in Europe until
the later decades of the thirteenth century, when, as de
Roover dubs it, a "commercial revolution"[3] occurred. Italian

---

[1]Gras, Business and Capitalism, pp. 115-16.

[2]Culled from R. Barlow, "Medieval Italian Merchants
and the Development of Accounting," unpublished term paper in
Business Administration 208, The University of Michigan, May,
1958, pp. 4-5.

[3]Raymond de Roover, "The Commercial Revolution of the
Thirteenth Century," in Lane and Riemersma, op. cit., pp. 80-
82.

merchants chose to become sedentary and no longer attend the
fairs of Champagne which had established that French province
as the commercial center of civilized Europe during most of
the twelfth and thirteenth centuries.

Spurred by the development of credit instruments such
as the bill of exchange, and by the increased safety along
the roads, merchants began to employ representatives, rather
than doing the traveling themselves. Where petty capitalists
had occasionally utilized the partnership form on a per-
voyage or per-trip basis, the sedentary merchant adopted a
terminal (usually for one, three, or five years) partnership
under which far-flung agencies were created. The merchant
could thus work with larger amounts of capital, yielding him
a wider span of control: from his counting-house, he directed
many activities which included importing and exporting, whole-
saling, retailing, transporting, communicating, storing, banking, insuring, and pawnbroking. Here was diversified enterprise in full flower. As the merchant enlarged the scope of
his activity, the old-line town began to disappear; metropol-
itan areas arose. As one writer states,

> The sedentary merchant was the key pin of the system.
> He was the great policy-formulator, manager, and con-
> troller. He laid the foundations of extended trade,
> big business, big cities, exploration, and general
> culture.[1]

Thus, stimulated in part by the potential of newly-
discovered international trade routes, and in spite of (1)
continual political conflict between Italian city-states and

---

[1] Gras in Lane and Riemersma, op. cit., p. 75.

the feudal lords of the rest of Europe, (2) numerous and uncertain taxes, and (3) monetary-unit instability, large commercial enterprises began to sprout. Foreign trade in Western Europe became virtually an Italian monopoly, for that
country dominated foreign trade in the Levant, Southern
Europe, France, Flanders, and in England.

Northern Europe as a commercial power was several
strides behind. Until the Elizabethan era (1558-1603),
England was commercially backward. By 1500, two centuries
of progress still separated the Hanseatic merchants from
those of Italy. Moreover, Sweden resembled a natural economy
until the sixteenth century. De Roover, citing this dispar-
ity in economic development, relates:

> Nothing brings out this fact more clearly than
> the crudeness of German methods of bookkeeping as
> compared with Italian methods. Hanseatic partner-
> ships were formed for a single venture or were loose
> associations involving one merchant operating from a
> certain trading center and another merchant from an-
> other center. In partnerships of the latter type
> the settlement of accounts was sometimes postponed
> for years. . . . The Hanseatic system of keeping
> books was more or less satisfactory as long as only
> two partners were involved, but it was entirely in-
> adequate when partnerships became three- or four-
> cornered affairs. Accounts would soon become hope-
> lessly entangled and lead to lawsuits and even to
> more serious difficulties [such as bankruptcies]. . . . [1]

For accountants, the major consequence of this commercial metamorphosis was the effective birth of systematic
bookkeeping. The factors contributing to this development
were many. With the increased use of agencies and credit

---

[1]De Roover in Lane and Riemersma, op. cit., p. 83.

instruments, inter-party relationships grew more numerous and complex. Particularly significant was the tendency of many a merchant to become a member in several partnerships, further complicating his financial status. Furthermore, the Arabic numerical system was introduced in Italy during the thirteenth century (but not in England until the late fifteenth century), although it did not receive widespread use for bookkeeping purposes until some two centuries later.[1] And finally, the rising "houses," or partnerships, of Southern and Central Europe--Bardi, Peruzzi, Alberti, Medici, Fuggers, Welsers, et al.--brought forward the need for partners to learn periodically their financial interest in the firm. Beyond these considerations, expert observers of Middle Ages business enterprise disagree. Historians attach varying degrees of significance to different phenomena. Yamey, for instance, minimizes the role of double-entry bookkeeping during these years. He appears to wonder why double-entry was even used this early, for he finds that the main uses to which it was put (inventory taking, a record of credit, a check by the owner on the existence of assets) could have well been satisfied by single-entry.[2] Sombart, on the other hand, views double-entry bookkeeping as the vehicle through which the

---

[1] Woolf, op. cit., p. 97; also see Werner Sombart, Der Moderne Kapitalismus (2 vols.; Leipzig: Verlag von Duncker & Humblot, 1902), I, 296.

[2] B. S. Yamey, "Scientific Bookkeeping and The Rise of Capitalism," in W. T. Baxter (editor), Studies in Accounting (London: Sweet & Maxwell, Limited, 1950), pp. 13-30.

growing depersonalization and rationalization--both being
essentials of full-grown capitalism--became effective.[1] Gras,
less enthusiastic, comments that Sombart's writings have been
"stimulating, popular, and influential," adding, however,
that "probably his theories will be discovered to be almost
all wrong."[2] Gras further warns that manuals and other treatises should not occupy too much attention of the researcher
who wants to grasp the significance of bookkeeping to enterprise of that day; Yamey, it seems, relies almost solely on
such evidence. Out of this discord over research techniques
and preconceived notions, therefore, it is difficult to piece
together the importance to developing business enterprise of
double-entry bookkeeping, and vice versa.

But the fact remains that double-entry bookkeeping
did appear that early, although there is evidence to indicate
that much less than its full potential was utilized. Moreover, despite the gradual depersonalization of enterprise
which accompanied the rise of Europe's family partnerships,
a "proprietary" view prevailed. Continuing restraints on
the profit goal oriented early double-entry bookkeeping more
toward "proprietary" capital and "proprietary" profit. Falke
accounts for the absence of the unbridled profit motive in
the family partnerships, as follows:

> Trading, for these families, was not just a
> means to acquire quickly and easily a fortune, after
> which the activity was transferred to other hands.

---

[1] Sombart in Lane and Riemersma, op. cit., pp. 37-40.

[2] Gras, Business and Capitalism, op. cit., p. 151.

On the contrary, commerce itself was a binding principle of these families; in a process of slow and
certain increase over the centuries commerce led to
the accumulation and preservation of the fortune of
a large kinship group. Commerce was the solid foundation of a high social position in the civic com-
munity. It was also, for the younger members, an
unfailing opportunity for instruction and honorable
action.[1]

Legitimate capitalism, in the Sombartian sense, was yet to

come.

Before proceeding, the "two faces" of double-entry

bookkeeping should receive attention. Undoubtedly, a sig-

nificant cause of the dissonance among historians about the

place of double-entry bookkeeping derives from lack of agree-

ment on what is meant by the phrase, double-entry bookkeep-

ing. One should distinguish between double-entry bookkeep-

ing in form and double-entry bookkeeping in substance. "In

form" implies bilateral accounts with a duality of entries;

only "real" accounts (asset, liability, and proprietorship)

are necessary here. "In substance," contrariwise, requires

additionally a "commercial proprietorship, and especially

those elements which are called 'nominal accounts' or 'econ-

omic accounts' [that is, expense and revenue accounts]."[2]

In short, double-entry bookkeeping in substance comprehends

the records necessary for determination of profit as well as

for the drawing up of the balance sheet. Although double-

---

[1]Falke, as quoted by Sombart in Lane and Riemersma,
op. cit., pp. 32-33.

[2]A. C. Littleton, Accounting Evolution to 1900 (New
York: American Institute Publishing Co., Inc., 1933), p. 27.
Yamey, it might be inferred, implies "double-entry bookkeep-
ing in substance" when discussing double-entry bookkeeping.

entry bookkeeping _in form_ doubtless found acceptance[1] as early as the fourteenth century, the more substantive version was to come _en masse_ sometime later.

Second, one should be aware of the possible interpretations of the word "entity." Nussbaum, for example, states that the establishment of capitalistic forms of business during the fifteenth through eighteenth centuries "was marked especially . . . by the notion of the business as an accounting entity."[2] Others, among them Sombart, also write of the accounting entity (or _ragione_) of the Middle Ages.[3] These writers are evidently calling attention to the attempts by merchants of that day to design bookkeeping systems for their firms. They do not pretend to imply that the accountant's "entity theory" began to replace the "proprietary theory," or if they do, the evidence does not support their thesis.

Double-entry bookkeeping _in form_ can be traced as early as 1340 to the records of the Commune of Genoa. With the growth of the sedentary merchant and his network of relations with others, the systematic set of records known today as double-entry bookkeeping undoubtedly attracted a large

---

[1] See, for example, Frater Lucas Pacioli, "De computis et scripturis." (Thirty-six chapters from _Summa de Arithmetica, Geometria, Proportione et Proportionalita_, Venice, 1494.) Translated by Pietro Crivelli. _An Original Translation of the Treatise on Double-Entry Book-Keeping by Frater Lucas Pacioli_ (London: The Institute of Book-Keepers, Ltd., 1924).

[2] Nussbaum, _op. cit._, p. 158.

[3] Sombart in Lane and Riemersma, _op. cit._, p. 37.

following. Control-conscious merchants of the later Middle
Ages found bookkeeping to be a valuable instrument, although
they made little real use of the potential which double-entry
offers.

The first treatises on double-entry bookkeeping,
however, were not written until the fifteenth century. Bene-
detto Cotrugli wrote a book entitled <u>Della mercatura e del
mercante perfetto</u> (Of Trading and the Perfect Trader), which
appeared in Venice in 1573, although a notation at the end
of the work suggests that it was completed 115 years earlier.
Lucas Paciolo,[1] a Franciscan friar and a well-known authority
on mathematics in his day, is credited with having been the
first to publish. Appearing in 1494, his work was entitled,
<u>Summa de Arithmetica, Geometria, Proportione et Proportionalita</u>
(Everything concerning Arithmetic, Geometry, and Proportion).
Most of his work was mathematical, thirty-six chapters on
bookkeeping (entitled <u>"De computis et scripturis</u>," or "Of
reckonings and writings") being appended only with the following apology for their inclusion in a dissertation on mathematics: "In order that the subjects of the most gracious Duke
of Urbino may have complete instructions in the conduct of

---

[1]Whether it is "Pacioli," "Paciolo," or one of some
dozen other spellings which are occasionally found, has generated a good deal of fine-tooth combing of the Italian's
manuscripts. Because (1) most historians prefer it (see
Littleton, <u>op. cit.</u>, p. 76), and (2) Boursy's conclusions
are persuasive in its favor, this writer has adopted "Paciolo."
See Alfred V. Boursy, "Name of Paciolo," <u>The Accounting Review</u>
(July, 1943), pp. 205-09. Cf. R. Emmett Taylor, "The Name of
Pacioli," <u>The Accounting Review</u>, XIX, No. 1 (January, 1944),
69-76.

business, I have determined to go outside the scope of this work and add this most necessary treatise."[1] To be sure, the title of Paciolo's volume does not even hint of a section on bookkeeping.

In expositing "the method employed in Venice,"[2] Paciolo describes a system which has retained its major outlines for almost 500 years. His record books are three: the Memorial, Journal, and Ledger. Because of the chaotic state of coinage during the Middle Ages, the money values of transactions needed a common denominator. Events were therefore first recorded in "raw form" in the Memorial, and later, when reduced to a standard unit, transferred to the Journal.

Paciolo writes of a "Profit and Loss" account, which, upon closing one ledger and opening the next, is to collect all balances that are not to be forwarded as such. The balance of Profit and Loss thence is closed to Capital. No mention is made of financial statements, but Littleton reminds us that they would have been redundant for the small proprietors of that day.[3] (But what of the large family partnerships?) In addition, the absence of "theory," that is, deductive reasoning from postulated principles and inductive reasoning from observed practice, is evident throughout Paciolo's thirty-six chapters. Such was true of virtually every bookkeeping work (hence the term "bookkeeping" is used

---

[1] As quoted in Woolf, op. cit., p. 113.

[2] Pacioli, op. cit., p. 2.

[3] Littleton, op. cit., pp. 84-85.

instead of "accounting") until the late nineteenth century.

Paciolo's exposition of "the method of Venice" must be studied carefully to determine whether real substance had been introduced into his double-entry bookkeeping. Does Paciolo represent a "break" from others' attempts to envelop the firm's "debitors" and "creditors" in a double-entry set of books—with only fleeting and sporadic attention to profit and loss? Although Paciolo shows some concern for profit, his version of profit determination appears to be only an incidental appendix to the balance-sheet type of bookkeeping which characterized that period.

It is admitted that the mechanics of the Paciolo double-entry system are fundamental to bookkeeping as now practiced and have weathered several centuries of economic change. But it is the flesh, not the bones, which must be placed in historical relief. These may appear to be harsh words for a man who is generally recognized as having published the first systematic presentation of double-entry bookkeeping. They are not offered in that tone. It is true that the basic Paciolo structure is still extant today. Not commonplace today, however, is Paciolo's central theme: to give the trader without delay information as to his assets and liabilities.[1] Clearly subsidiary to this goal, in Paciolo's construct, is profit determination. The latter is a dynamic

---

[1]Cited as Paciolo's main purpose by Richard Brown, A History of Accounting and Accountants (Edinburgh: T. C. & E. C. Jack, 1905), p. 111, and by Woolf, op. cit., p. 113. Woolf's volume, by and large, appears to be a condensation of Brown's pioneering work.

process whereas the former--keeping track of assets and lia-
bilities--is an exercise in comparative statics.

This is not to criticize Paciolo or the Venetian
method, though neither is above criticism. If the trader
of that day placed first priority on information relative to
assets and liabilities, the Paciolo system would serve well.
Brown, for one, thinks it did, stating that "at the close of
the fifteenth century . . . the 'method of Venice' was developed to a state which exactly met the requirements of that
period."[1] Accountants today would call this method "the balance-sheet approach." It also typifies the "proprietary"
concept in that it deals with the proprietor's capital and,
when calculated, the proprietor's profit: the business entity
was treated merely as a conduit for the proprietary viewpoint.

But before passing final judgment on Paciolo, let us
mark closely his comments on "closing" and the "Profit and
Loss account." "Balancing of the book," which culminates
in the transferring of account balances from the old ledger
to the new ledger occurs

> . . . when you want to change book [sic] by reasons
> of its being filled up, or because of the beginning
> of a new year, as it is customary to do in the best
> known places. The big merchants always observe this
> custom every year, specially in the New Year.[2]

---

[1]Brown, ibid., p. 119.

[2]Pacioli, op. cit., p. 90. This writer has been unable to determine the nature of Paciolo's distinction between
"new year" and "New Year." The Geijsbeek translation suggests a far different meaning than Crivelli's "New Year."
Geijsbeek's relevant passage reads: ". . . as is customary in
the best known places, especially at Milan where the big

Brown recounts, however, that the "practice of not making a general balance till the ledger was completed [was] widespread till the seventeenth century."[1] Such was the frequency of the closing process. Some evidence exists, on the other hand, to indicate that a profit figure was drawn annually by some merchants, even without a balancing (that is, closing) of the books.[2]

As to the nature of profit determination, Paciolo recommends that "those accounts which you may not desire to transfer to Ledger A [that is, the new ledger], but which you wish to keep privately, and have no obligation to render an account of to anyone" should be closed to Profit and Loss.[3] Among these accounts might be "mercantile expenses, household expenses, all extraordinary expenses, rents, pensions, [and]

---

merchants renew every year their Ledgers." J. B. Geijsbeek, as quoted in Littleton, op. cit., p. 68.

[1]Brown, op. cit., p. 107.

[2]Nicolo Barbarigo, a Venetian merchant, made an annual profit calculation between 1456 and 1482, though he closed the books but once during the 27 years. Brown, ibid., p. 107. Cotrugli, in his 1458 manuscript, gives directions for the annual closing of Profit and Loss to Capital. Manzoni (1534) reports that in many places bookkeepers ruled the accounts and began new books each year. Littleton, op. cit., pp. 211-12 (footnote). Paciolo, of course, observes in an above-quoted sentence that the calculation of an annual profit was "customary . . . in the best known places." Yamey does not appear convinced, however, that profit was computed very often. Even if it were so computed, he probably would argue, the figure was probably not used in the merchant's business decisions. See Yamey, op. cit., pp. 13-30, and B. S. Yamey, "The Functional Development of Double-Entry Bookkeeping," The Accountant, November 2, 1940, pp. 333-42.

[3]Pacioli, op. cit., p. 98.

feudal tributes."[1] The Capital account, once having received the balance of Profit and Loss, would "always enable you to know the value of your whole property. . . ."[2] Occasionally remarking that the keeping of expense accounts and Profit and Loss would disclose how the business was progressing, Paciolo nonetheless interprets profit determination as subsidiary to balance-sheet aspects of bookkeeping. In fairness to Paciolo, one must observe that practically all record-keeping of his day was with Roman numerals; this fact alone might severely restrict the facility with which any set of books might be used. In these circumstances anyone who would propose a bookkeeping system which approximates the scope of the present-day system is brave, indeed.

"After Paciolo," writes de Roover, "accounting entered into a period of stagnation which lasted until the nineteenth century."[3] This statement is true with respect to changes in bookkeeping technique, but it does not gainsay another important role which bookkeeping was about to play. Bookkeeping, it will soon be seen, was a major enabling factor in the ascendancy of the capitalistic system.

The progress of bookkeeping during the sixteenth century consists primarily of the diffusion of Italian bookkeeping throughout Europe. In 1543, Ympyn introduced the Italian method to Flanders by publishing a book which was clearly a

---

[1]Ibid.   [2]Ibid., p. 99.

[3]Raymond de Roover, "New Perspectives on the History of Accounting," The Accounting Review, XXX, No. 3 (July, 1955), p. 418.

transcription of Paciolo's; by 1547, it had been translated
into French and English.[1] Also, in 1543, Hugh Oldcastle published a translation of Paciolo in English--the earliest known
bookkeeping treatise in that language. That Oldcastle was a
teacher of arithmetic as well as of bookkeeping comes as no
surprise. Many of the sixteenth-century published expositions of bookkeeping appeared in mathematics treatises. This
relationship implies that bookkeeping might have been too
abstruse for the average merchant, further implying that
Paciolo's double-entry may have been more written about than
practiced. That this conclusion may not be wholly valid is
suggested by H. M. Robertson, who cites Ympyn's publication
as "of great moment in the spread of economic activity and
the spirit of capitalism."[2] Double-entry was both cause and
effect. In the thirteenth century a capitalistic innovation
(that is, the sedentary merchant) had contributed significantly to the launching of double-entry bookkeeping. In the
sixteenth and seventeenth centuries, however, double-entry
bookkeeping helped build a fire under capitalism. "One cannot say," writes Sombart of the entire sweep of events,
"whether capitalism created double-entry bookkeeping, as a
tool in its expansion, or whether perhaps, conversely, double-
entry bookkeeping created capitalism. . . ."[3]

---

[1]Brown, op. cit., p. 130.

[2]H. M. Robertson, Aspects of the Rise of Economic In-
dividualism: A Criticism of Max Weber and His School (Cambridge,
Eng.: The University Press, 1933), p. 56.

[3]Sombart in Lane and Riemersma, op. cit., p. 38.

Once Holland became familiar with Paciolo's method,
that country "remained the leading country in accounting
standards."[1] In the seventeenth century, over 400 works on
bookkeeping were published in the Dutch language.

But bookkeeping technique developed slowly. As the
anti-profit ethical constraints of Southern Europe began to
evaporate, the pursuit of unlimited gain became honorable.
Capitalism could thus advance, for acquisitiveness (or profit
seeking) is its most important objective. The spread of
double-entry bookkeeping through Europe played no small part
in the rise in stature of this profit motive. "There is no
doubt that reliance on good books [that is, adequate bookkeeping records]," puns Robertson, "meant more than reliance
on the Good Book."[2] He adds that "it would be very easy to
substitute systematic books for the Protestant ethic as the
origin of the capitalist spirit."[3] With this, Max Weber
agrees.[4]

Influence of the Corporate Form

Another determinative set of events was taking shape.
The seeds of the modern corporation--probably second only to
the rise of the sedentary merchant in impact on bookkeeping
practices--were being sown in Northwestern Europe. In re-

[1]Nussbaum, op. cit., p. 161.

[2]Robertson, op. cit., p. 56.

[3]Ibid.

[4]Weber's concurrence is noted at ibid.

sponse to the rapid extension of commerce to distant lands
after the mid-1500's, specially-licensed prototypes of the
corporation sprung up. The British East India Company, established in 1600, raised funds on the familiar per-voyage
basis; but the Dutch East India Company, thought to be the
first stock corporation, was organized two years later with
a permanent capital. By 1612, it is interesting to note,
the British company had begun to issue stock on a more permanent basis--doubtless emulating its counterpart across the
Channel. Littleton suggests that an important reason for
the British company's gradual changeover to permanent capital
was the demonstrated inadequacy of bookkeeping methods to
straighten out the distributive shares at the end of each
voyage.[1] In 1657, the British company secured a new charter
making it a full-fledged permanent stock company.

During the seventeenth century, particularly because
of the ascent of the Stuarts (with James I in 1603), stock
corporations flourished in England. The Stuarts helped form-
ulate the so-called "fiat doctrine," whereby the crown could
grant special privileges and monopolies to corporations,
which would come to be viewed as fictitious legal persons
apart from their officers or members. On the Continent, corporations also grew in importance, but the doctrine of legal
entity, never as strong as in England, was discarded under
the Code Napoléon.

---

[1]Littleton, op. cit., p. 211.

The heyday of English corporations reached an abrupt
end in 1720, however, when the South Sea "bubble" burst after
a hectic period of promotion and speculation.[1] The Bubble
Act of 1720 circumscribed the conditions under which stock
corporations, then the subject of public disfavor, could be
created. A similar bubble-bursting in France did much to
dampen Continental enthusiasm for the corporate form. The
stock corporation was resigned to lie in a paralytic state
until a new economic stimulus could rejuvenate its limbs.
That stimulus, it turned out, was the Industrial Revolution.

By the end of the seventeenth century, English bookkeeping was characterized by a "roping off" of permanent capital and by periodicity. In 1661, as an example, the British
East India Company's governor announced that future distributions would consist of profits earned--dividends rather
than "divisions."[2] Thus we see one of the first corporate
demands upon bookkeepers for a periodic determination of
profit and the separation of accumulated profit from permanent capital. These developments, according to Littleton,
were prompted more by the conditions of the time than by the
influence of Italian bookkeeping. The earlier speculative
manias were instrumental in this regard. Writes Max Weber,
"Not until the 18th century did the annual balance and inventory become established customs, and it required many

---

[1]A. A. Berle, Jr. and Gardiner C. Means, "Corporation,"
in Seligman and Johnson, *Encyclopaedia*, IV, p. 415.

[2]Littleton, *op. cit.*, p. 211.

terrible bankruptcies to force their acceptance."[1]

Aside from the delineation of capital from income, bookkeeping, according to Yamey, made little progress during those years. The vast majority of enterprises, Yamey observes, used single-entry until well into the nineteenth century. Although the early "balance account" (that is, balance sheet) was first discussed in a textbook in 1546,[2] merchants apparently did not use it except for gathering account balances when the ledger was filled.[3]

The Profit and Loss account was used to collect assorted unimportant asset balances that were not to be carried forward. It was a repository, as Yamey puts it, for "refuse and dregs."[4] A hodgepodge, it included dowries, household expenses (also mentioned by Paciolo), money lost or won in lotteries, and personal drawings. "There is little evidence," writes Yamey, "of a careful calculation and analysis of profits, and even less of any attention to the separation of business from domestic affairs."[5] The textbooks emphasized other uses of bookkeeping data in preference to the analysis of profit and (surprisingly) of financial position. Double-entry seems to have become popular because "it

---

[1]Max Weber, General Economic History (Glencoe, Ill.: The Free Press, 1927); translated by Frank H. Knight; p. 282.

[2]Littleton, op. cit., pp. 125-26.

[3]See Yamey, "Scientific Bookkeeping," op. cit., pp. 13-30, and Yamey, "The Functional Development," op. cit., pp. 333-42.

[4]Yamey, "Scientific Bookkeeping," ibid., p. 25.

[5]Ibid.

rendered the taking of subsequent inventories superfluous."[1]

The Coming Of Industrial Capitalism

Adam Smith's magnum opus,[2] improved transportation, and the pervasive Industrial Revolution launched what Sombart calls "the era of full capitalism."[3] Although historians differ, this period probably extends from 1750 to shortly before 1900--earlier in Great Britain than in the United States.

The debut of coal and iron, and the steam engine, together with increased war and luxury demand, specialization of labor, and intensive price competition--all made for a mass market demand and mass production.[4]

Given the right to protect inventions by patents, businessmen could parlay new ideas with mass production techniques in order to build large and profitable enterprises. The corporation was the natural vehicle for the enlargement of the scale of enterprise. Here were the mental attitudes and organizational framework within which Schumpeter's entrepreneur could generate the cyclical economic development which is indigenous to capitalism.

Sombart's requisites for capitalism are essentially

---

[1]Yamey, "The Functional Development," op. cit., p. 338.

[2]Adam Smith, An Inquiry into the Nature and Causes of the Wealth of Nations (New York: The Modern Library, 1937).

[3]Sombart in Seligman and Johnson, Encyclopaedia, III, p. 203.

[4]Weber, op. cit., chap. 27.

three: acquisitiveness, enterprise autonomy (which embraces
"depersonalization"), and rationalization.[1] Various relax-
ations in the strictness of religious and ethical tenets, together with the get-rich-quick lures of foreign lands, assisted in elevating to the level of respectability--if not pop-
ularity--the profit-maximization goal. (As noted above, the
ubiquity of double-entry bookkeeping added to this profit
fever.) Enterprise autonomy was supplied by the corporate
form. And bookkeeping is the sine qua non of rationalization. But rationalization, like the other two, is a mandatory requirement. Without rationalization, "capital" is an
empty concept. Without rationalization, acquisitiveness
loses operational meaning and exists only as a kind of pro-
pensity--as if the wind were known to be blowing but there
was no way to measure its velocity. Capitalism requires all
three conditions; the presence of only two will not produce
a two-thirds result.

Thus it should be plain that evolving mental attitudes
and means of business organization interacted with the spread
of record-keeping techniques to produce fully-grown capitalism. As far as bookkeeping is concerned, it remains for its
practitioners and teachers to determine the most effective

---

[1]To rationalize, according to Sombart, is to reduce
a metaphysical or abstract notion to concrete, measurable
dimensions. For instance, the concept of capital may be
rationalized by expressing a quantum of capital. Only through
rationalization of relevant economic factors, Sombart thought,
could they be made operational. Bookkeeping is thus the
means of rationalizing capitalistic activity.

and useful _means_ of rationalization.

To return to the historical development of the corporate form, which is of particular interest to accountants,
one notes that the post-Bubble revival of stock corporations
was slow. During the eighteenth century, England chartered
only six corporations for manufacturing purposes.[1] Not until the Companies Act of 1844 did the licensing of stock
corporations, other than for canals, become common. Further,
limited liability was denied corporations in England until
1855. Nonetheless, the widespread British use of the joint
stock company seems to have sufficed during the early 1800's.

The _Code de commerce_ of France, in 1807, ultimately
served as a model for the rest of the continent. It provided
for the _société anonyme_ (share corporation), but specific
authorization therefor was required from the government until
an 1867 act liberalized the law.

In America, despite fear of the corporation (together
with the monopolies they often represented) which had been
engendered by the hostile activities of British companies,
the corporation reached an advanced state earlier than was
true abroad. By 1811, New York State had enacted the first
general incorporation law. Such laws were common by 1850,
and in 1865, when the growing railroads asked for permission
to issue preferred stock over a layer of already-existing
common, the permission was granted. Berle and Means describe

---

[1]Oscar Handlin and Mary F. Handlin, "Origins of the
American Business Corporation," in Lane and Riemersma, _op.
cit._, p. 104.

this newly-found authority as "the germ of the modern conception of corporate power--the belief that the rights of the participants as well as the technical conduct of the business must be subject to managerial discretion."[1] The development of the large corporation was made even more feasible by the state legislatures of Delaware, Maryland, and Nevada, which allowed their domestic corporations to exercise a wide range of powers.[2]

Although the evolution of the corporation intensified the demands on bookkeeping for a separation of capital from income, the absence of conceptual discussion of the subject by accountants (as they might now be called) kept them on the defensive. English statutes did not define income, leaving its determination to the courts. Some nineteenth-century English courts, for example, decreed that corporate profit was the excess of the current value of the assets over liabilities (including capital contributed).[3] Therefore, an essentially accounting question devolved on the legal profession; it is wholly conceivable that the existence of a well-reasoned accounting position on this matter might have influenced the courts' decisions. As it was, there was none. Had accountants written earlier on the conceptual underpinnings of their discipline, there might be

[1]Berle and Means in Seligman and Johnson, Encyclopaedia, IV, p. 417.

[2]Ibid., p. 418.

[3]Littleton, op. cit., p. 216.

fewer differences today between accounting and legal interpretations of financial data.

Corporation statutes of the nineteenth century forced,
directly and indirectly, the expansion of the scope and--ul-
timately--the theoretical depth of accounting. Mere bookkeeping (that is, the record-keeping procedures) needed substantive content. It was enlarged into accounting when its
practitioners and teachers ended their reticence and under-
took an active discussion of the conceptual justification of
its role.

Summary and Conclusions

In retrospect, double-entry bookkeeping arose for a
number of reasons, the least important of them being the purpose for which bookkeeping is today used: the preparation and
analysis of financial statements. But what were the causes
of its development? It is impossible to comprehend them all,
or even to assign an appropriate "weight" to each. Double-
entry's completeness and orderliness must have caught the
fancy of many. Scholarly minds appear to have been attracted
by its abstractness. The feeling of having conquered a somewhat complex computational problem rewarded others, including
Edward Thomas Jones, who wrote in 1795:

> To Balance a set of Books at the first trial
> appears wonderful, and is mentioned with astonish-
> ment; and for the same person to do so two or three
> years following, he is said to possess a portion of
> infallibility, and is freely allowed to boast of
> the exploit as long as he lives.[1]

---

[1]Quoted in Yamey, "The Functional Development," op.
cit., p. 341.

Double-entry assisted merchants in keeping track of
debts and inventory. A merchant might have felt better that
some record was being kept of his business affairs rather
than have none at all--even though he would not want much
information from it.

But ironically, the profit and loss statement and (to
a lesser extent) the balance sheet--as separate financial
statements--are of relatively recent origin, though double-
entry bookkeeping has been practiced for over four centuries.
"The theoretical implications of [profit] were probably never
given a thought," writes Yamey of early bookkeeping.[1] And
the balance account was only a mere incidental, performing
purely technical functions.

Bookkeeping was both a cause and effect of the coming
of capitalism. Although bookkeeping was a necessary ingred-
ient of capitalism, one might query whether--after the triumph
of the latter--bookkeeping maintained the pace of capitalism.

More appropriate to this study is another question:
Does the use today of the basic outlines of early Italian
bookkeeping also require the continuance--to be consistent--
of the Italians' proprietary approach? Or has the gradual
evolution of the capitalistic economy brought with it the
need for a new pair of spectacles?

Accountants finally began to think seriously about
these questions not much more than a half century ago, which
proves that although bookkeeping is old, accounting is still

---

[1] Ibid., p. 339.

young.

Subsequent chapters will trace the development of accounting thought on these questions.

CHAPTER III

THE EVOLUTION OF THE ACCOUNTING PROCESS TO
1900, WITH PARTICULAR REFERENCE TO ITS
INTERRELATION WITH THE ORIENTATION
POSTULATE

The previous chapter outlines the parallel development of capitalism and the bookkeeping process. It is the
aim of this chapter to trace the apparent evolution of the
accounting process up to the beginning of the twentieth
century.

Since the latter part of the fifteenth century, when
Paciolo's treatise appeared, the character of the accounting
process appears to have developed at an uneven pace; the
factors which have acted to re-shape the accounting process
have had only an ambiguous relationship with particular
changes in the process itself. For example, as will be indicated below, the advent of the corporation, together with
the Industrial Revolution, had a profound effect on the
accounting process. Nonetheless, it is very difficult (if
not impossible) to determine the exact sequence of causal
changes in the accounting process which were occasioned by
each.

History consists of crosscurrents of political, social,
and economic phenomena which cannot be unequivocally sorted

as to causes and effects as might be done where controlled
laboratory conditions are available. It is true that bookkeeping procedures have changed relatively little since
Paciolo.[1] But the purposes for which these procedures have
been employed, the principles dictating the manner in which
the procedures are to be applied to economic data, and the
principles setting forth the kinds of data that are relevant
to the determination of whatever result is sought have under-
gone a marked change. It is these latter three characteristics which comprise the accounting process--as distinct from
the bookkeeping process (that is, the mechanical steps according to which the data are assembled, classified, and prepared
for analysis).[2]

Like the bookkeeping process, the accounting process
has responded to fundamental political and economic changes.
Inasmuch, however, as pre-twentieth-century treatises on
accounting and bookkeeping rarely discussed matters of theory,
the reasoning behind the development of accounting principles

---

[1]Littleton agrees. See A. C. Littleton, Accounting
Evolution to 1900 (New York: American Institute Publishing
Co., Inc., 1933), p. 84.

[2]In a book review of H. J. Eldridge, The Evolution
of the Science of Book-keeping, contained in Accounting Research, Vol. V, No. 4 (October, 1954), 368-69, C. E. Hall
states that "book-keeping is the maintenance of books for recording transactions and accounts; accountancy is the application of these results for any particular purpose that is
required." Accountancy, or accounting, comprises the questions of substance, while bookkeeping comprises the questions
of procedure and mechanics. For emphasis, "accounting process" is here used as a synonym for accountancy, thus defined.
The above quotation is from p. 368.

must be inductively derived from the available data. To a
significant extent, therefore, the material in Chapter II
will be drawn upon as a basis for this evolutionary study.

Definitions and Terms

In describing the accounting process, accountants
use the terms "proprietary theory" and "entity theory."[1]
They are not theories, however; they are alternative assumptions upon which other theories may rest. A theory is "a
general principle, formula, or ideal construction, offered
to explain phenomena. . . . [It is] an analysis or explanation."[2] Indeed, one may theorize as to which assumption is
the more appropriate. But they themselves are not theories,
for they explain nothing.

At this point the meanings of several technical terms,
instrumental in describing the "scientific approach," should
be introduced. They are: technique, procedure, convention,
principle, concept, postulate, and hypothesis. A. C. Little-

---

[1]Among the many accounting writers who refer to the
"entity theory" or "proprietary theory" are Stephen Gilman,
Accounting Concepts of Profit (New York: The Ronald Press
Company, 1939), especially chap. 5; Littleton, op. cit., es-
pecially chaps. 11, 12; George Hillis Newlove and S. Paul
Garner, Advanced Accounting, Vol. I: Corporate Capital and
Income (2 vols.; Boston: D. C. Heath and Company, 1951), chap.
1; Morton Backer, "Determination and Measurement of Business
Income by Accountants," in Morton Backer (editor), Handbook
of Modern Accounting Theory (New York: Prentice-Hall, Inc.,
1955), pp. 207-47; and William J. Vatter, "Corporate Stock
Equities--Part I," in Morton Backer, ibid., pp. 359-83.

[2]Webster's New International Dictionary of the English
Language (Springfield, Mass.: G. & C. Merriam Company, 1957),
Unabridged, Second Edition, p. 2620.

ton and Noah Webster (that is, the current revision of his
original work) will serve as authorities:[1]

technique - "a skillful way of acting"; "the manner of
            performing." (Littleton, p. 141)

procedure - "a sequence of operations by which account-
            ing techniques are applied with a common
            objective"; "a group of techniques."
            (Littleton, p. 141)

convention - "a customary rule, regulation or require-
             ment that is more or less arbitrarily es-
             tablished by common consent or tacit under-
             standing." (Littleton, p. 142)

principle - "an explanation . . . [which compresses] an
            important relationship among accounting
            ideas into a few words." (Littleton, p. 146)

concept - "a mental pattern of related ideas which grow
          into an integrated complex idea as more and
          more relevant instances become known"; " in
          relation to principles, accounting concepts
          may be the point of origin of some principles,
          or may be a composite of a group of principles";
          "a family group of principles." (Littleton,
          p. 148)

---

[1] A. C. Littleton, Structure of Accounting Theory (Urbana, Ill.: American Accounting Association, 1953), Monograph
No. 5; and Webster's, op. cit. Hereinafter in this chapter,
Littleton, Accounting Evolution to 1900 and Littleton, Structure of Accounting Theory will be referred to, respectively,
as "Littleton, Evolution" and "Littleton, Structure."
    For discussion by logicians of the nature of a "pos-
tulate," see C. West Churchman, Elements of Logic and Formal
Science (Chicago: J. B. Lippincott Company, 1940), pp. 10-11;
and Daniel Sommer Robinson, The Principles of Reasoning: An
Introduction to Logic and the Scientific Method (New York:
Appleton-Century-Crofts, Inc., 1947), p. 362.
    Notwithstanding the contention that postulates should
not be subjected to critical examination, it would appear to
be necessary as well as desirable that theoretical structures
not be erected until their foundations are determined to be
sound. The validity of principles and concepts, it would seem,
is no greater than the validity of the assumptions, or postulates, that underlie them.

postulate - "an assumption that provides the first premise in a train of reasoning"; "an underlying
hypothesis." (Webster, p. 1931)

hypothesis - "a tentative theory or supposition previously
adopted to explain certain facts and to guide
in the investigation of others." (Webster,
p. 1230)

The reasoning behind the matching of costs with revenues constitutes a concept, within which the reasoning that
underlies the determination of cost is a principle.

Preparatory to the application of concepts or principles to a particular problem, several postulates may need
to be developed. How shall the data be organized and interpreted? What orientation and perspective should the analysis
take? In short, the postulates describe the environment in
which the analysis (employing concepts and principles) is to
be performed.

The position that the business enterprise should be
viewed as a part of the proprietor's person constitutes a
postulate. In turn, it affects the nature and orientation of
the subsequent analysis. In the fifteenth century, this postulate was also a convention (in the broad sense of that
term). That income should be calculated each year is a rule.
(It has postulate-like characteristics in that it may influence succeeding analysis, but it is not properly described
as an "assumption.") Today, it is also a convention. Principles and concepts, within a framework of postulates and
rules, explain the justification (or lack thereof) of procedures and techniques.

On what basis, one may ask, should postulates be
formulated? The Special Committee on Research Program of
the American Institute of Certified Public Accountants concludes the following:

> Postulates are few in number and are the basic
> assumptions on which principles rest. They neces-
> sarily are derived from the economic and political
> environment and from the modes of thought and cus-
> toms of all segments of the business community. . .
> The principles, together with the postulates, should
> serve as a framework of reference for the solution
> of detailed problems.[1]

Moreover, postulates should be determined interdepen-
dently. They are necessarily interrelated and mutually dependent. The collection of postulates (and rules) should be
internally consistent, else the succeeding analysis may contain discordant strains. Consequently, the modification of
a postulate (or a rule) may have repercussions on other postulates (and rules) as well as on principles and concepts.

Because of the possible implications for other postulates[2] and principles and concepts of a change in one postulate, it would not be unnatural for one to be mindful of
the numerous principles, concepts, and other postulates with
which a given postulate is consistent when he speaks of that
given postulate. More specifically, if one attempts to explain the entity postulate, he might (by design or not) in-

---

[1] American Institute of Certified Public Accountants,
"Report to Council of the Special Committee on Research Program," in The Journal of Accountancy CVI, No. 6 (December,
1958), p. 63.

[2] Hereinafter, except where specifically kept separate, "postulates" shall comprehend rules as well as postulates.

clude therein the principles, concepts and other postulates
with which he believes the entity postulate to be in harmony.
Newlove and Garner, for example, list 14 "tenets" of each of
two alternative formulations of a postulate.[1] (That they
label each alternative as a "theory" undoubtedly contributes
to their belief that each is a theoretical synthesis in itself.) These authors evidently include the entire superstructure of principles, concepts, and other postulates within the
ambit of a single postulate.

Throughout this study, the entity and proprietary
points of view will be regarded as postulates, although substitute words (for example, view, viewpoint, approach) may
also be employed. One must be cautious not to allow substitute terms (which may have only an imperfect synonymy with
the correct term) to carry broader and thus misleading conno-
tations of what is meant. One writer refers to the entity
(or proprietary) postulate as variously a concept, theory,
viewpoint, approach, and convention--all within the space of
two pages.[2] The latter three terms are probably harmless
substitutes, but "concept" and "theory" imply much more than
does a postulate.

With this definitional and terminological discussion
as a background, an examination of the historical development

---

[1]Newlove and Garner, op. cit., I, 21-22.

[2]Gilman, op. cit., pp. 49-50.

of the proprietary and entity postulates may be attempted.

Outline of the Analysis

Below it will be demonstrated that accounting writers differ among themselves as to the denotation of each of the two postulates. It would seem that the definitional confusion could be significantly reduced if each term were traced to its earliest applications. By this process, the broad outlines of the evolution of the accounting process may be more clearly demarcated. It will be seen that the accounting period convention, the orientation postulate (that is, proprietary or entity), the valuation principle and the matching concept--each influencing one or more of the others-- grew up together. Collectively, they attempt to answer the following questions about the nature of the accounting process:

1. What is the appropriate frame of reference within which economic data should be studied and toward which economic data should be oriented? Possible answers are: the accounting unit (a) as an abstract being; (b) as an extension of the owner's personality inclusive of the owner's other affairs; or (c) as an extension of the owner's personality, but separately considered from the owner's other ventures or household activities. In brief, is the business enterprise more appropriately envisaged as possessing a separate existence or as being a satellite within its owner's sphere of activities? The answer to this question, essentially one of choosing a perspective, will necessarily condition the manner

in which accounting data are to be organized and interpreted.[1]

2. What evaluative criteria are appropriate for measuring quantitatively the significance to the accounting unit
of its changing asset composition? If one accepts the economist's position that it is the function of business enterprise to assist in the efficient allocation of scarce resources, in what manner should the resource allocation be studied?
What is the proper conceptual framework for tracing the appear-
ance and disappearance of various asset quanta? Further,
what factors should be weighed (and in what proportions) in
determining profit? Tangentially, one must ask whether the
assets should be viewed as belonging to the proprietor or to
the firm. Implicit in this question is a choice between the
proprietary and entity postulates.

3. What is the appropriate time span for which accounting determinations should be made? Possible answers are:
(a) the life of the owner, (b) the life of the business enterprise, or (c) a time segment which is less than the life
of either. The latter choice may suggest (i) the time necessary for production and delivery of a product, (ii) a "natural"
business cycle of the business enterprise, or (iii) a time interval otherwise selected. What, then, should be the accounting calendar?

Evidently, a given answer to any of the above ques-

___

[1]For agreement, see Backer, "Determination and Measurement of Business Income by Accountants," in Backer, op. cit.,
pp. 213-14.

tions might carry profound implications for most of the others.[1] Their answers need to be jointly determined in order to achieve a harmonious and internally consistent body of theory. Utilizing this indicative (as opposed to definitive) inquiry into the requirements of a "body of accounting theory" as a point of reference, we are now ready to examine the episodes in its historical development.

Development Prior to the Corporation

Perhaps the earliest evidence of formal bookkeeping is the records of Roman slaves.[2] Viewing amounts owed to his master as debts rather than as ownership claims, the slave exhibited an entity-like preference for his economic role. In that a principal-agent relationship, in contradistinction to a proprietor-business firm relationship, existed between master and slave, the term "entity-like" is preferred over "entity." After all, the slave was not an inanimate organism, and is not unlikely to have seen himself as an "entity."[3]

The slave, it seems, generally was to execute short-term buy-and-sell, wholesaling-type transactions, or he might be occupied mainly with investing the master's surplus wealth in commercial loans. Moreover, there would have been little ground for dispute over alternative methods of asset valua-

---

[1]See footnote 1, p. 50, and ibid., p. 211.

[2]See Chapter II, pp. 13-14, and Gilman, op. cit., chap. 4.

[3]For agreement, see Gilman, ibid., p. 39.

tion, for if a $100 purchase, later marked up on the books
to $160, were sold for $120, the master would nonetheless be
ahead by $20. The master had no one but himself to satisfy.
The recording of revaluations hence would add nothing new to
his comprehension of the economic facts. Were an accountable
manager placed between the master and slave, however, that
manager might well have been wary of valuations other than
original cost; such valuations might pervert his record of
stewardship. But in fact no such go-between was used in the
typical master-slave arrangement; the master was his own manager. He had complete control. Revaluations in this kind of
setting were therefore unlikely to arise.

With the renascence of active commercial enterprise
and of formal bookkeeping following the early Middle Ages,
came differently-organized business activity. The merchant,
trading on his own behalf, became interested in the fluctua-
tions of his ownership equity.

Most of what is known today about medieval bookkeeping comes from Paciolo.[1] From his account of "the method of
Venice," together with a few other writings, it may be concluded that: (1) the merchant did not regard his enterprise
as a separate entity; (2) he seems to have preferred the
"historical cost" method of asset valuation, with exceptions;
(3) he computed profit (if at all) at irregular intervals,

---

[1] See Chapter II, especially pp. 24-31.

often not until his ledger was full; and (4) he was interested more in the balance of his capital (that is, equity) account than he was in revenues, expenses, and profit--as such.[1] Related discussion follows:

(1) The separateness of the business enterprise. Perhaps at no other time in the history of formal bookkeeping has the business firm been viewed as less a separate entity than in the medieval era. If the opposite number of the "entity postulate" be dubbed the "proprietary postulate," bookkeeping during the Middle Ages evinced an indisputable proprietary character. A few quotations from Paciolo support this view:

> We cannot do without recording the ordinary household expenses [in the merchant's books]. By this is understood such expenses as grains, wines, wood, oil, salt, meat, boots, hats, coat fashioning, under-waistcoats, stockings, tailor expenses, drinks, tips, barbers, bakers, water-carriers, woollen cloths, kitchen utensils, vases, glasses, windowpanes, and all the buckets, baths, tubs, and barrels.[2]
> If you should desire you may include with these household expenses all extraordinary expenses, which you do not usually take notice of, that is, when you spend money in playing various kinds of games, or money or things which you might lose, or may be stolen from you, or lost at sea or through fires, etc., for all are intended to be extraordinary expenses, which, if you desire you may keep separately, as many persons do, in order to know clearly at the end of the year how much they have spent as extraordinary expenses,

---

[1] For a full discussion of the meaning of this distinction, see footnote 1, p. 64.

[2] Frater Lucas Pacioli, "De computis et scripturis." (Thirty-six chapters from Summa de Arithmetica, Geometria, Proportione et Proportionalita, Venice, 1494), translated by Pietro Crivelli. An Original Translation of the Treatise on Double-Entry Book-Keeping by Frater Lucas Pacioli (London: The Institute of Book-Keepers, Ltd., 1924), p. 66.

and in which should also be included gifts and presents that you may make to anyone for any reason.[1]

Indeed, medieval practice went even beyond the "proprietary theory," for the latter implies that business and household affairs are kept separate for accounting purposes. Hence, not only was the enterprise not accorded the center of accounting attention, it was in effect given no attention at all. In this factual setting, it is probably of little value to refer to the "proprietary theory" and "entity theory" in their usual senses, for each presumes a separate accounting for business and household affairs. Nonetheless, given the merger in the accounts of business and household transactions, the medieval merchant, as will be noted in more detail below, looked to the balance of, and changes in, his capital account for indications of his status and progress, respectively. In this way, the merchant adopted a kind of proprietary approach. The "entity theory," for purposes of this chapter, shall imply the existence of the business enterprise as a separate and accountable unit for accounting purposes.[2]

---

[1] Ibid., p. 67.

[2] Because of the medieval merchant's mixture in the accounts of business and personal affairs, the terms "proprietary theory" and "entity theory" can be utilized, at best, in a somewhat awkward manner in connection therewith. The reader should therefore be aware that they are used rather loosely in this chapter. In the section, "A Re-examination of the Multiple Phases of the Orientation Postulate," in Chapter IV, a more precise delineation of the various conceptions of the orientation postulate is presented.

This mixture of personal and business data may well have been brought about by the methods of fifteenth-century taxation. Particularly in the first decades of that century a very heavy tax was levied on citizens' property.[1] It is not unlikely that a tax on combined business and household property prompted merchants to merge their business and household records.

This condition cannot provide the entire explanation, however. Business enterprise was small. The trader could not help but identify himself with the vehicle of his gainful pursuit, and there were no legal concepts of "business entity" to remind him to the contrary. He was owner and manager. He was the firm. (In the case of the typical partnership,[2] all of the partners appear to have participated actively in its affairs. Again, there was little or no separation of ownership and management.) If the trader were inclined to seek justification in economic theory for his role, he would have found little (if any) guidance; the theory of the firm and of the related price system had not yet been born. Indeed, barter was still common in his day. If he could have conducted a depth interview of medieval merchants to learn why they mentally commingled their household affairs with those of their business enterprises, this writer would expect

---

[1] See A. C. Littleton, "Genealogy for 'Cost or Market,'" The Accounting Review, XVI, No. 2 (June, 1941), p. 162.

[2] Partnerships of that day were usually of only short duration. Littleton, Evolution, p. 137 (footnote).

56

them to express bewilderment that any other view was tenable.

Interestingly enough, Paciolo says almost nothing about the use to which his accounts might be put. He offers only very little discussion of possible inferences and no comments whatsoever as to possible analyses which might be drawn therefrom. As to inferences, he states: "Said Capital Account, which should always be last in any Ledger, will always enable you to know the value of the whole of your property, providing you add the debits and credits which you have transferred to Ledger A."[1] Paciolo's Profit and Loss account, as noted above, is closed directly to Capital,[2] indicating that his profit (or, more correctly, the Venetian merchant's profit) was seen as an adjunct not to the enterprise as a whole, but to the owner's equity. Hence the net change during the period which he would single out for emphasis is the accretion to (or declination in) the owner's equity. Consistent with this, he places emphasis on the owner's equity account (as opposed, for instance, to total resources) as the important gauge of the firm's status. And when he says ". . . the value of the whole of your property,"[3] the bookkeeping records become merely a vehicle through which the merchant can ascertain the worth of his combined personal and business possessions. Paciolo stresses not the value of the

[1]Pacioli, op. cit., p. 99.

[2]Ibid., pp. 98-99.

[3]Emphasis supplied. See footnote 1 for citation.

enterprise, but the value of the merchant's equity in the
enterprise.[1] In sum, Paciolo describes a method which is
built around the merchant, not the enterprise. The separate
existence of the enterprise was in effect denied; further,
the accounting view of the merged unit was "proprietary"--
that is, seen through the eyes of the proprietor.

(2) The method of valuation. Paciolo seldom refers
to asset revaluations in his treatise, but offers a "criterion" for determining which values should be transferred to
the new ledger. His "criterion," if it is deserving of this
term at all, is highly subjective: "Those accounts which you
may not desire to transfer . . . but which you wish to keep
privately, and have no obligation to render an account of to
anyone . . . should be closed."[2] Accounts which Paciolo believed to fit this description were "mercantile expenses,
household expenses, all extraordinary expenses, rents, pensions, [and] feudal tributes."[3] Accounts which he would
usually carry forward were "cash, capital, goods, furniture
and buildings, debtors, creditors, offices, brokerages, and
dues to public weighers."[4]

Paciolo gives relatively little attention to monetary
values. He deals mostly with account titles, not monetary
amounts within the accounts. Paciolo on several occasions,[5]

---

[1]These two values cannot be the same except where no
debt exists. Paciolo discusses debt matters in his chap. 18.

[2]Pacioli, op. cit., p. 98; emphasis supplied.

[3]Ibid. [4]Ibid. [5]Ibid., chaps. 12, 16.

however, recommends the use of current prices for the inventory of a new business; in one passage he suggests that the inventory value be "rather higher than low; that is should they appear to you as worth 20, put them down at 24. By this means you will obtain a better profit."[1] Whether he intends to say that a higher closing inventory valuation is translated into a higher current profit or that a high current profit would result by exhibiting this ledger balance to prospective buyers (he relates elsewhere[2] that many merchants kept duplicate books, one set being for display to buyers who were to accept the inventory values as "cost") is not clear.[3] It is nonetheless clear that when opening the ledger for a new enterprise, Paciolo prefers a current-price valuation. But Paciolo recommends that the inventory be carried from the old ledger to the new at its carrying value in the former.[4]

To the extent, however, that fifteenth-century enterprise was transient and not relatively enduring, it would appear that the use of current-price revaluations--as opposed to the relating of costs to revenues--would be more suitable to the determination of the change in proprietary capital.

---

[1]Ibid., p. 27.   [2]Ibid., p. 18.

[3]For further discussion on this point, consult Lawrence L. Vance, "Authority of History in Inventory Valuation," The Accounting Review, XVIII, No. 3 (July, 1943), 221, footnote 5; and Littleton, "Genealogy," op. cit., p. 163.

[4]Pacioli, op. cit., p. 100. For an interpretation of Paciolo's comment, see Richard Brown, A History of Accounting and Accountants (Edinburgh: T. C. & E. C. Jack, 1905), p. 118.

Although it appears that the relatively stable family partnership was the predominant business form in at least the
Venetian Republic,[1] a multitude of large-scale, limited-term
ventures nonetheless were characteristic of the day. In
addition, there were numerous small-scale ventures, as there
are today. But "big business" of the Middle Ages was carried
on by both permanent family partnerships and short-term joint
ventures.

Had the accounting records and reports of that day
been prepared on a basis consistent with today's standards of
disclosure, the medieval joint venture would have required
periodic current-price revaluations for profit-determination
purposes--for the assumption of continuity, or going concern,
would ostensibly not have applied to these kinds of undertakings.[2] Yamey, for one, strongly implies that had the results of the medieval accounting process been more preoccupied
with "profit," current-price revaluations would have been in

---

[1]See Frederic C. Lane, "Family Partnerships and Joint
Ventures in the Venetian Republic," in Enterprise and Secular
Change, ed. Frederic C. Lane and Jelle C. Riemersma (Homewood,
Ill.: Richard D. Irwin, Inc., 1953), pp. 86-101.

[2]For an elaborate treatment of this point, see pp.
99-104   of Chapter IV.
The following comments by Nammer are of interest: "In
the middle-ages, the single venture was the dominant form of
business organization. Liquidation rather than going concern
was the characteristic of such enterprises." Helmi Mahmoud
Nammer, "An Activity Concept of the Business Enterprise and
Its Implications in Accounting Theory" (unpublished Ph.D.
dissertation, Graduate College, University of Illinois, 1957),
p. 154. Nammer does not document his first statement.

order.[1] As it was, he notes, "Description of assets [for inventory-taking purposes] appears to have been much more important than their 'quantification.'"[2]

The significance, in relative terms, of the limited-term venture in the medieval economy would seem to justify the argument that a valuation method that is consistent with the assumption of "imminent termination of the concern" (as opposed to "going concern") would have had far more relevance then than it has today. That medievals did not use such a method, or inquire into its feasibility, is not necessarily indicative of its inapplicability to businesses of the time. Rather, their inaction in this respect should be interpreted as only one of many consequences of their attitude toward the usefulness of the results of double-entry bookkeeping. They did not seek the financial insights that are sought today; hence, their methods--together with the theoretical development relative thereto--could be comparatively simple and loose-jointed. The medieval period will therefore be conceived as one in which a current-price approach might have justifiably received wide usage.

Three separate instances of "lower of cost or market" are reported to have occurred in the first dozen years of the

---

[1] B. S. Yamey, "Scientific Bookkeeping and The Rise of Capitalism," in Studies in Accounting, ed. W. T. Baxter (London: Sweet & Maxwell, Limited, 1950), p. 24.

[2] Ibid.

fifteenth century.[1] Although Littleton implies[2] that the
high Italian property tax may have been the major inducement
for traders to have minimized inventory values, Vance contends (to the contrary)[3] that taxes and inventory values had
little connection and that "lower of cost or market" was used
mainly to improve the quality of profit determinations.

Use of current prices appears to be consistent with
the medievals' proprietary approach. To a "proprietary" advocate, the balance-sheet equation was

Assets - Liabilities = Proprietorship,

as opposed to

Assets = Liabilities + Proprietorship

or

Assets = Equities.[4]

To be sure, Cronhelm's formulation,

Positive properties - Negative properties = Proprietor's stock,[5]

more suggests the interaction of assets (positive properties)
and liabilities (negative properties) which is characteristic
of the proprietary approach. The change in proprietorship

---

[1]Littleton, "Genealogy," op. cit., p. 162.

[2]Ibid., pp. 162-63.

[3]Vance, op. cit., pp. 219-21. One might criticize
Vance's suggestion that a more perfect profit figure was the
goal (or even an important goal) underlying the use of "lower
of cost or market." Medievals exhibited little interest in
profit qua profit; their concern was with establishing a quantum which would reflect their total worth.

[4]Littleton, Evolution, pp. 169-70, 192.

[5]Ibid., p. 170; for further discussion pertaining to
F. W. Cronhelm, see below, pp. 90-91.

(that is, the capital account), it would follow, is derived
from the changes in assets and liabilities. The value of
liabilities, being the amounts owed, could usually be found
readily. The value of the assets would be found by inventory-
ing the assets on hand and by applying thereto their current
prices. The use of current prices thus would seem to be
wholly consistent with the objective of finding the amount
of the proprietor's equity--it being the excess of the current value of what he has over the amount which he owes.
(These amounts included, it should be noted, all of his properties, business and otherwise, and all of his debts.)

Depreciation accounting was non-existent then--it
continued to be a rarity until the late nineteenth century.
Fixed assets played a minor role in those old books.[1]

(3) The regularity of profit determination. It was
noted above[2] that the formal calculation of profit was not
the yearly ritual which it is today. Paciolo does, it is
true, exhort the trader to close his ledger each year, "especially he who is in a partnership as the proverb says--
frequent accounting tends to lasting friendship."[3] But an
annual closing (usually the only time at which a formal profit
calculation was made) appears to have been the exception, not
the rule.

Whether merchants developed informal profit computa-

---

[1] Ibid., p. 85.

[2] Chapter II, pp. 27-28 and footnote 2, p. 28.

[3] Pacioli, op. cit., p. 84.

tions cannot be determined. It seems unlikely that they would not have kept a close check on their capital account (or, less likely, their profit and loss account), whether the books were closed or not. Nevertheless, two major factors have acted to obscure the nature and scope of medieval book-keeping procedure. First, heavy taxes on personal property caused traders to keep their business affairs, and particularly their records (other than those that were purposely exhibited to buyers), behind a curtain of secrecy--in order to avoid paying any greater a levy than tax officials could determine for themselves. Hence, whatever financial statements, formal or informal, which Italian traders drew up were certain not to be advertised. Second, the relative infrequency of credit transactions and the general condition of owners being their own managers foreclosed the necessity of "external reports." Moreover, textbooks of the fifteenth and sixteenth centuries were usually written by mathematicians and school teachers; whether the methods they espoused also received widespread usage is very difficult to determine; seldom did practitioners write on the subject. Partnerships and bankruptcies appear to have provided much of the historical evidence of medieval bookkeeping practice.

(4) Emphasis on capital account or profit. It is clear from Paciolo's statement of the object of bookkeeping[1]

---

[1]Paraphrased, his object is: to give the trader without delay information as to his assets and liabilities. For reference to the source of this statement, see p. 26 and footnote 1, p. 26, of Chapter II.

that emphasis was then placed on balance-sheet data, as opposed to income-statement data.[1] His description of the closing process, quoted above,[2] relegates the profit figure to a position behind that of the capital account balance.

Partnerships, which were the dominant form of enterprise in the fifteenth and sixteenth centuries (in Italy),[3]

---

[1]Rather than speak of "balance sheets" and "income statements," reference is made to data--as they would be contained in each of these media. For formal financial statements appear to have been nonexistent in that day.

Perhaps it would be even more accurate to say "balance-sheet-oriented data as opposed to income-statement-oriented data." Successive balance sheets necessarily impart the same essential financial information as would intervening income statements. The two financial statements are logically interdependent and interconnected; their difference is chiefly temporal, the balance sheet being an expression of an accounting unit's financial status while the income statement is an expression of the accounting unit's financial progress. The former is stationary or static; the latter is moving or dynamic. Nonetheless, each income-statement period must possess a beginning and an end. A comparison of balance sheets, one each prepared at the beginning and at the end of that time period, would naturally disclose the changes which have occurred in the interim. Thus, income-statement data inexorably find their way to the balance sheet--but in static terms. In accounting jargon, revenues and expenses are but mirror-reflections of the changing composition (as a result of pursuing the business objectives of the firm) of the firm's assets (and liabilities).

When one refers, therefore, to a shifting of emphasis from one financial statement to the other, he intends to say merely that dynamic- rather than static-oriented data (or vice versa) are more relevant to the user's purpose in wanting the statements. It is the point of view rather than the inherent nature of the data which would cause one statement to take precedence over the other.

[2]See Chapter II, pp. 25-28.

[3]For authority, see Lane in Lane and Riemersma, op. cit., pp. 86-101, especially p. 86.

required a careful record of the partners' capital. The
occasion of a partner's withdrawal from membership necessi-
tated a computation of the retiring partner's capital balance.

The delicate partnership relation, incidentally,
appears to have been a prime force behind the early development of financial statements. The "balance account," an
informal summary of the account balances after closing, was
a forerunner of the modern-day balance sheet, although the
former seems to have been found in the ledger itself and not
as a separate document.[1]

> Another strong motive for the separation of financial
> statements was the settlement of partnership affairs.
> The closing of the books would not always suffice,
> for then only the one having the books would preserve
> a record of the situation at the moment.[2]

Favoritism toward "balance-sheet data," however, is
evident. Littleton concludes that

> the primary motive for separate financial statements
> was to obtain information regarding capital; this was
> the center of the interest of partners, shareholders,
> lenders, and the basis of the calculation of early
> property taxes. Thus balance-sheet data were stressed
> and refined in various ways, while expense and income
> data were incidental--in fact, the latter in the sev-
> enteenth century were presented merely as a 'proof of
> estate'--to demonstrate by another route the correct-
> ness [sic] of the balance-sheet.[3]

Summary and Conclusions

In review, what can be said about the accounting of

---

[1] For discussion of early "balance accounts," see
Littleton, Evolution, pp. 127-32.

[2] Ibid., p. 137.

[3] Ibid., p. 153.

this period? Virtually all accounting was a private matter,
that is, for the owner-manager's use alone, although tax
assessors apparently utilized accounting data to the extent
that records were available. But legal interposition was
minimal; firms appear to have been largely free from governmental dicta.

Merchants merged their business and personal affairs
into the same set of books in order to ascertain therefrom
the worth of their entire property. Inasmuch as proprietors
could examine their bookkeeping records for information as
they needed it, the closing process and the consequent computation of a net increase in the capital account were put off
until a full ledger required a transferring of account balances to a new book. Financial statements as we know them
today were not needed, and therefore, not prepared.

The valuation of assets seems to have varied among
firms, and any one firm might use different methods for different assets depending on the desired result. In short, no
ground rules existed for asset valuation and (conjointly)
profit determination. The accounting treatises of the day
concentrated almost solely on bookkeeping methods.

Profit determination was clearly ancillary to the
computation of the capital account balance. Whether this
was true because inventory valuation was haphazardly accomplished or whether inventory valuation was haphazard because
few people cared about the profit figure, is impossible to
tell.

But one general conclusion seems justified. The view that the business enterprise is personal to the owner-manager seems to have fostered a casual, informal approach to the formulation of financial measures of the firm's position and progress. An attitude of "anything goes" prevailed, and the resulting change in capital was derived according to a conglomeration of rule-of-thumb procedures which reflected a diversity of objectives. Profit was a catch-all measure; it had no conceptual underpinnings; it was simply a residue, and was interpreted as merely a preliminary calculation toward the ascertainment of the new capital balance.

This attitude toward financial measurement probably would not have been so easily facilitated by the entity approach.[1] Viewed as an accounting entity, the firm is accountable to its capital-suppliers; it follows that arm's length accounting analyses would have emerged from this entity-to-entities relationship.[2] Instead, the medievals' use of the

---

[1]The medievals' version of the proprietary postulate being more in harmony with the economic climate of the times (small firms, owners being managers as well), one should not infer that the entity approach was then a real alternative to that which was used. Business enterprise was personal to its owners. Adoption by medievals of the entity postulate is advanced only as a conjecture, to contrast the nature of financial reporting which is the product of the proprietary approach with that of the entity approach.

[2]It is admitted that any proprietor, if he is typical of the "economic man" (that is, in search of profit maximization), would hold his firm accountable for its accomplishments. It is only contended here that use of the entity postulate is more conducive to explicit accountability of the firm. Although the proprietor may in fact treat the firm as an accountable unit, his acceptance of the proprietary postulate may not permit any outward manifestation of such accountability. According to all outward appearances, the firm and

proprietary postulate in effect denies the firm's separate
existence, and conceives of it as an appendage to the proprietor's sphere of activity. Being a dependent, the firm,
like a child, is not held accountable for its actions. Only
the proprietor has reached his majority; only he is responsible, and he, after all, is the personification of the firm.
What the firm does is also his doing, and the umbilical cord
(so to say) between the firm and the proprietor is his capital account. It is the one nexus which is common to both.
Whatever ground rules which the proprietor should wish to
establish for the measurement of his interest in the firm
are personal to him and need not reflect the economic efficacy of the firm's operations.

The absence of substantial creditor equities during
medieval times further insulated the firm from the need for
being accountable.

It will be shown that it is no mere coincidence that
the gradual adoption of the entity approach was accompanied
by more coherent and internally consistent standards for
financial measurement. To be sure, the economic and political conditions which commended use of the entity postulate
also brought about the necessity for more forthright finan-

---

the proprietor would be viewed as one; any arm's length accountability would appear to be absent. Acceptance of the
entity postulate, on the contrary, would produce a climate
of dispassionate inquiry engendering a more objective and ex-
acting genre of accountability. The third-party nature of
the entity approach would seem, therefore, to encourage a
fuller and more effective accountability.

cial reporting. Among these were the introduction of income taxes, the advance of the corporate form, the Industrial Revolution, and the growing interest of governmental regulatory bodies in business. By these developments, the business firm --principally the corporation--attained maturation. It became accountable (in a formal sense) as a separate being. As an accounting entity, it required a new approach to the Sombartian rationalization for depicting its economic accomplishments. Thereupon, the firm was required to justify its existence--not only in brain impulses to its nerve center (that is, the proprietor) but in clear and unambiguous language to an assortment of interested parties. It was the need for this kind of financial communication that precipitated the rigorous development of the principles of profit determination.

Advent of the Corporation

A more systematic and economically defensible (as will be shown) approach to the derivation of accounting analyses was to reach fruition only after (1) the business enterprise came to be viewed as an accounting entity and hence accountable to third parties, or (2) the business enterprise grew so large in size or complexity that the owner (or manager) had to rely on statistical evaluations of its progress and status. A legal phenomenon, the corporation, and an economic and social phenomenon, the Industrial Revolution--each interacting upon the other--arrived in the eighteenth and nineteenth centuries to satisfy requirements (1) and (2).

Although the modern concept of the corporation was not legally recognized until the nineteenth century,[1] the joint stock company (regarded by Ballantine as the true fore-runner of the modern corporation)[2] began to grow roots in the early 1600's. The joint stock company differed from the (general) partnership in that all of the former's members usually did not participate actively in the business. For the first time, therefore, an element of absentee ownership appeared. Accountability to the inactive investors was needed.

The early history of the giant British East India Company has already been sketched.[3] It will be recalled that the Company was granted a permanent-stock charter in 1657. By the terms of this document the Company's stock was to be valued first at the end of seven years and thereafter at the end of every three years.[4] This provision, coupled with the governor's aforementioned pronouncement,[5] gave to accounting

---

[1]In England, the first general law was the British Companies Act of 1862. In the United States, numerous states enacted early laws which, in one or more ways, resembled the "general act" of today. Among the earlier general-type acts were those of New York, 1811 and 1849; Massachusetts, 1829; Connecticut, 1837; and Ohio, 1846. See Chelcie C. Bosland, Corporate Finance and Regulation (New York: The Ronald Press Company, 1949), p. 24; and Adolf A. Berle, Jr., Studies in the Law of Corporation Finance (Chicago: Callaghan and Company, 1928), ch. 1, especially p. 20.

[2]Henry Winthrop Ballantine, Ballantine on Corporations (Chicago: Callaghan and Company, 1946), Revised Edition, p. 33.

[3]See above, Chapter II, pp. 32-33.

[4]Littleton, Evolution, p. 211.

[5]Chapter II, p. 33 and footnote 2.

its first inducement to develop a body of principle for the determination of periodic profit. As Littleton observes:

> Italian double-entry bookkeeping, already well
> developed and in a sense awaiting its destiny,
> afforded the organic mechanism for accomplishing
> the careful separation of these two elements, cap-
> ital and income, under most diverse and, as future
> centuries were to demonstrate, unexpected circum-
> stances. The joint stock companies (corporations)
> were the catalyst in whose presence the permanent
> investment of capital assets was united with the
> mechanism for measuring income.[1]

Accounting in a Corporate Society

The corporate form as created by statutory law[2] had three direct effects and one indirect effect on accounting development. First, corporation law endowed a business un- dertaking with a distinct personality--"a legal unit, a con- cern separated off with a legal existence, status or capacity of its own. . . ."[3] The corporation, being a legal unit, became a natural candidate for consideration as an account- ing unit.

Second, the grant of limited liability to corporations prompted legislators to provide for some measure of protec- tion for creditors. Corporation laws thus stipulated that a

---

[1]Littleton, Evolution, p. 213.

[2]As Berle points out, various corporate forms existed for centuries prior to the time when they became "creatures of the law." Berle, op. cit., chap. 1.

[3]Ballantine, op. cit., p. 2. For a concise discus- sion of some of the various legal theories of the corporation, see Richard Goode, The Corporation Income Tax (New York: John Wiley & Sons, Inc., 1951), pp. 9-13.

certain part of the owners' investment be deemed inviolate.[1]
In order to maintain this capital buffer, it became necessary
to restrict the equity source of ordinary corporate distributions to stockholders. Dividends could therefore not be
"paid" from legal capital in the ordinary course. They might
only come from profits. May quotes Lord Campbell in "one of
the earliest of the English dividend cases" (1849):

> Dividends are supposed to be paid out of prof-
> its only, and when directors order a dividend, to
> any given amount, without expressly saying so,
> they impliedly declare to the world that the com-
> pany has made profits which justify such a dividend.[2]

Indeed, this case was decided prior to the enactment by Parliament of the first Companies Act which restricted the source

---

[1]This designated amount, usually called "legal capital,"
was originally viewed as a trust fund in favor of creditors.
Wood v. Dummer, 3 Mason 308, Fed. Cas. No. 17,944 (C. C. Me.
1824); Sawyer v. Hoag, 17 Wall. 610 (1873). This conception
of legal capital has since been displaced by the "fraud theory."
Hospes v. Northwestern Mfg. & Car Co., 48 Minn. 174 (1892).
Nevertheless, a specified portion (usually the par value of
issued shares, or, when the shares have no par, an amount stipulated by the directors) of stockholders' investment must be
kept safe from impairment. For further discussion, including
other relevant cases, consult Prosper Reiter, Profits, Dividends and the Law (New York: The Ronald Press Company, 1926),
pp. 87-89; Donald Kehl, Corporate Dividends (New York: The
Ronald Press Company, 1941), chap. 2; Ballantine, op. cit.,
pp. 803-08; and Laylin K. James, Cases and Materials on Business Associations (Indianapolis: The Bobbs-Merrill Company,
Inc., 1949), Second Edition, pp. 358-87.

[2]Quoted in George O. May, "External Influences Affecting Accounting Practice," a talk given before the International
Congress on Accounting, New York City, on September 11, 1929.
Reproduced in Proceedings, International Congress on Accounting (New York: 1930), pp. 686-97, at p. 693.

of dividends to profits.[1] Littleton succinctly describes

the chain of logical bridges between the corporation and

(its impact upon) accounting:

> . . . the separateness of the corporate entity pro-
> vides the logic behind limited liability in corpor-
> ations; limited liability brings about the positive
> legal and equitable obligation to preserve invested
> capital intact from the encroachments of dividends;
> restriction of dividends in turn makes necessary the
> careful calculation of profit, including allowance
> for depreciation; and in accounting (bookkeeping ex-
> panded under the pressure of new responsibilities)
> is found the instrument par excellence for analyzing
> and recording the occurrences of business in such a
> manner as to make possible a fair computation of
> available profit.[2]

Third, corporate law provided for a regular reporting

of corporate progress and status (at first, only the latter

was emphasized) to stockholders. Hence, the periodicity rule

which had up to then received only sporadic acceptance became

firmly rooted in corporate accounting.

The British Companies Act of 1862, which was the first[3]

---

[1]This "restriction" was contained in Article 64 of
Table B, an apparently optional set of model articles of incorporation contained in the British Companies Act of 1856.
Article 64 was the same as Article 73 (see below) in the 1862
Act. The Joint Stock Companies Act of 1844 provided only that
dividends may not come from capital. See H. C. Edey and Prot
Panitpakdi, "British Company Accounting and the Law, 1844-1900,"
in A. C. Littleton and B. S. Yamey, Studies in the History of
Accounting (Homewood, Ill.: Richard D. Irwin, Inc., 1956), pp.
356-79, especially pp. 356-62; and Littleton, Evolution, pp.
291-92.

[2]Littleton, Evolution, p. 257.

[3]Previous British acts pertained either to particular
branches of commerce (for example, banking, insurance, canal
companies) or permitted only varying degrees of limited liability. The 1862 Act consolidated the earlier laws and appears
to have been applicable to commerce generally. Thus, although

general corporation act of that country[1] to embody the modern
corporate concept, contained a model form for the "Memorandum
of Association" (that is, the by-laws) which, although not
obligatory upon companies which were created under the Act,
nevertheless came strongly recommended.[2] (At the very least,
the wording therein indicates the legislative policy of the
day.)[3] Relevant articles of Table A, as the model by-laws
were titled, are as follows:

> 73. No dividend shall be payable except out of
> the profits arising from the business of the company.
> . . . .
> 79. Once at the least in every year the direc-
> tors shall lay before the company in general meeting
> a statement of the income and expenditure for the
> past year. . . .
> 80. The statement so made shall show, arranged
> under the most convenient heads, the amount of gross
> income, distinguishing the several sources from which
> it has been derived, and the amount of gross expendi-

---

the choice is perhaps an arbitrary one (depending on one's
definition of "general"), the 1862 Act is interpreted as being the first "general act."

[1]For early U. S. "general acts," see footnote 1, p.
70, supra.

[2]Companies could choose their own by-laws, although
it appears (see supra, p. 72 and footnote 2) that some of
the principles embodied in the model by-laws had been adopted
by the English courts.

[3]But see Pixley, who writes: "No provision, however,
was made in [the 1862 Act] for the audit of accounts, although a schedule [that is, Table A] was attached. . . .
"The omission of all reference to the presentation
of Accounts to shareholders . . . in the Act of 1862, is
most extraordinary, when eighteen years previous it was evidently considered that legislation on this subject was desirable." The 1844 Act, Pixley continues, required "the
proper keeping of Accounts, the balancing of the books, the
preparation of a Balance Sheet, the audit of the same, and

ture, distinguishing the expense of the establishment, salaries, and other like matters. Every item
of expenditure fairly chargeable against the year's
income shall be brought into account, so that a just
balance of profit and loss may be laid before the
meeting; and in cases where any item of expenditure
which may in fairness be distributed over several
years has been incurred in any one year, the whole
amount of such item shall be stated, with the addition of the reasons why only a portion of such expenditure is charged against the income of the year.
    81. A balance sheet shall be made out in every
year, and laid before the company in general meeting,
and such balance sheet shall contain a summary of the
property and liabilities of the company, arranged under the heads appearing in the form annexed to this
Table. . . .
    82. A printed copy of such balance sheet shall
. . . be served on every member. . . .[1]

Several articles concerning the nature of the annual audit of

accounts were also included in the Table.

    Of no small significance in the evolution of the cost

principle of valuing inventories and relatively long-lived

assets was a 21-word qualifying statement included in the bal-

ance sheet "form" attached to Table A. Specifically, the

statement (which is underscored here) appeared as follows in

Part III of the "Property and Assets" section:

---

the reporting thereon by the Auditors. . . ." Francis W.
Pixley, Auditors: Their Duties and Responsibilities under
the Companies Acts and Other Acts of Parliament (7th ed.;
London: Henry Good & Son, 1896), p. 8. Note that mention
of a Profit and Loss Account, or the like, was omitted even
from the 1844 Act.
    The mandatory audit, it may be noted, was reinstated
by the Companies Act of 1900.

    [1]Reproduced in A. Glynne-Jones, The Companies Acts,
1862 to 1900 (London: Jordan & Sons Limited, 1902), pp.
156-58.

PROPERTY AND ASSETS.

III. PROPERTY held   SHOWING:-
      by the Company.   7. Immovable property, distinguishing-
                              (a) Freehold land
                              (b)   "   buildings
                              (c) Leasehold   "
                           8. Movable property, distinguishing-
                              (d) Stock-in-trade
                              (e) Plant

                              The cost to be stated, with
                              deductions for deterioration
                              in value as charged to the
                              reserve fund or profit and
                              loss.[1]

Beyond Article 80 in the optional by-laws, no attempt at de-
fining "profit" was essayed. Hence, the matter of working
out a body of principle upon which "profit" could be determined was left to the courts. And, as noted above, the pau-
city of theoretical writings in accounting caused the entire
profits question ab origine to be settled by the judiciary.

     The above-quoted articles indicate the influence
which evolving company law had on accounting. The particular qualifying statement on asset valuation was unequivocal
in its preference for "cost." The provision for "deterioration" was novel (although, of course, it had also appeared
in the 1856 Act); indeed, Edey and Panitpakdi note that this
provision goes even further than do those (which were mandatory) of the 1948 Act.[2] Once again, however, the members of
Parliament did not set down in the Act any meanings of the

---

[1] Ibid., p. 161.

[2] Edey and Panitpakdi, "British Company Accounting and
the Law, 1844-1900," in Littleton and Yamey, op. cit., p. 366.

two key words, cost and deterioration.

The Indirect Effect

Corporations had a major indirect effect on accounting. An ideal vehicle for the aggregation of large sums of capital--insofar as this aggregation became economically and technologically feasible in the wake of the Industrial Revolution--the corporation thus enabled business enterprise to grow to proportions which indicated the need for greater reliance on a more scientific approach to business management. The principles of "scientific management," launched and nurtured by such men as Taylor, Emerson, Gantt, Fayol, and Gilbreth, evolved as a result of the increasing complexity of business enterprise.[1] And the growth of cost accounting contributed in no small way to the pace of the "scientific management" movement.

The emergence of cost accounting, a phenomenon of the last quarter of the nineteenth century, furthered the use of cost--in preference to market value--for inventories.

---

[1] For a contemporary discussion by a noted economist of the "scientific management" movement, consult Alfred Marshall, Industry and Trade (London: Macmillan and Co. Limited, 1923), Fourth Edition, Book II: chaps. 11-12; for his treatment of the cost accounting aspect of the movement, see pp. 365-66. For two very considerable sources on the historical evolution of cost accounting, see David Solomons, "The Historical Development of Costing," in David Solomons (editor), Studies in Costing (London: Sweet & Maxwell, Limited, 1952), pp. 1-52; and S. Paul Garner, Evolution of Cost Accounting to 1925 (University, Ala.: University of Alabama Press, 1954).

The pioneering work of Garcke and Fells in 1887,[1] together
with the writings of other accountants and engineers, opposed
the use of market values because their use would cause the
anticipation of profits and thus be unconservative. Agreement on cost (or market, whichever is lower) as the method
for inventory valuation was reached in England during the
first few years of this century.[2] That country was about
ten years ahead of the United States in this respect,[3] because the Companies Acts (see above) were forthright in their
preference for (1) the cost method (as opposed to wholesale
use of market values without regard to cost) and (2) annual
audits.

Probably most influential in establishing the cost
principle in the United States were federal income-tax legislation and judicial interpretation thereof. The 1918 law
embodied the "completed transaction" and "cash or its equiv-
alent" principles in an apparent quest for objectivity.[4]
Several Supreme Court tax decisions, particularly the historic

---

[1]Emile Garcke and J. M. Fells, Factory Accounts, Their
Principles and Practice (London: Crosby, Lockwood and Son,
1887). "Factory Accounts was by far the best known English
work on costing to be published during the last quarter of the
nineteenth century . . . and it reached seven editions by 1922."
David Solomons, "The Historical Development of Costing," in
David Solomons, op. cit., p. 35.

[2]Garner, op. cit., chap. 10.

[3]Ibid., pp. 316-20.

[4]American Institute of Accountants, Changing Concepts
of Business Income, Report of Study Group on Business Income
(New York: The Macmillan Company, 1952), pp. 25-26.

Eisner v. Macomber opinion,[1] reinforced the notion that income, to be taxed, must first be realized. They contributed
significantly to the building-up in accounting literature of
what the Study Group calls the "so-called 'traditional cost
principle.'"[2]

Another trend, the increasingly wide dispersion of
corporate ownership during the first three decades of the
twentieth century,[3] brought about a more marked separation
of ownership from management. The accountant was thus required to address management's reports of accountability to
a more amorphous audience of owners. And the several governmental regulatory bodies which were created from 1887 to
1934 (particularly the Interstate Commerce Commission, Federal Power Commission, and Securities and Exchange Commission)[4]

---

[1]252 U. S. 189 (1920); see p. 207. The 5-4 decision,
written by Justice Pitney, adjudged that stock dividends were
not "income" within the meaning of the income tax statute.
Also see Changing Concepts, p. 27.

[2]Ibid.

[3]See Adolf A. Berle, Jr. and Gardiner C. Means, The
Modern Corporation and Private Property (New York: Commerce
Clearing House, Inc., 1932), Book I: chap. 4.

[4]Although the Federal Power Commission was created
under the Federal Water Power Act (1920), its authority at
that time was limited to the licensing of hydro-electric pro-
jects. Its membership then consisted of the Secretaries of
War, Interior, and Agriculture. The broadening of its authority to cover utility accounting and security issuances was accomplished by Parts II and III of the Federal Power Act (1935).
For elucidation, see Clair Wilcox, Public Policies Toward
Business (Chicago: Richard D. Irwin, Inc., 1955), chaps. 10
(securities regulation), 20 (public utilities), 21 (railroads),
and 22 (transportation in general).

prodded accounting groups into endorsing many changes.[1]

Hence, the direct and indirect effects of the coming of the modern corporation profoundly influenced the nature of the accounting process. Not only was the corporation an entity at bar. Because of the movement toward wider distribution of ownership, the corporation became separate in fact from its owners. The late-nineteenth-century tendency toward holding companies and early-twentieth-century wave of mergers and consolidations in the United States[2] served additionally to remove the center of corporate decision-making from the majority of stockholders.

Furthermore, although a very slow trend had been evident since the mid-eighteenth century, business enterprise had suddenly taken the posture of a continuing operation. Equipment and machinery came to dominate the asset structure of many corporations. In Paciolo's day, business enterprise usually consisted of one or more distinguishable undertakings: a voyage or a caravan. At the conclusion of such a venture, a profit (as then calculated) could be unambiguously assigned

---

[1]George O. May, Financial Accounting, A Distillation of Experience (New York: The Macmillan Company, 1943), especially chap. 14. Regulatory commissions have not always been in the vanguard of accounting progress. In recent years, certain anachronistic accounting regulations of the Interstate Commerce Commission were under investigation by a House committee; they had been criticized by a leading public accountant as having done "vicious damage" to the public. U. S. House of Representatives, Subcommittee on Legal and Monetary Affairs of the Committee on Government Operations, Hearings, Railroad Accounting Procedures (Prescribed by the Interstate Commerce Commission), 85th Cong., 1st Sess., April 30, May 1-3, 1957; see especially the reproduction of an address by Leonard Spacek, "Professional Accountants and Their Public Responsibilities," pp. 253-59; above quotation taken from p. 257.

[2]Berle and Means, op. cit., chap. 3.

81

thereto. By contrast, Hatfield writes:

> But to-day business is a continuum. Machinery
> serves for many years, the factory building stands
> for a generation, the railroad is built to last
> for ever. The industrial process is made up of a
> never-ending stream of raw materials, goods in pro-
> cess and finished commodities. Expenses are in-
> curred in common and not like the expenses of a
> caravan solely in connection with one parcel of
> goods. But man is strangely agricultural in his
> tradition, even though society has become industrial.
> Time was when the recurring cycle of the year was of
> immense significance to him, for seed-time and har-
> vest each came in connection with the course of the
> earth around the sun. And man still thinks that he
> must reckon results in terms of the accidental period
> involved in such a circuit. We demand to know how
> much a concern makes in a year. We must know, because
> the reciprocal rights of preferred and common stock-
> holders may be altogether changed, depending on whe-
> ther profit is to be attributed to the month of Decem-
> ber or to the following January. We must know in
> order to satisfy the demands of the income-tax collec-
> tor. And so accountants are asked to perform the
> hopeless task of taking this economic continuum, of
> chopping it up into arbitrary and meaningless lengths
> called a year, and apportioning to each such year a
> proper part of the cost of a building which will last
> fifty years, of a machine which will be used for
> twenty years, of a blast furnace which will last ten,
> and of a stock of coal bought in December which will
> all be consumed before spring again appears.[1]

Legal Entities and Accounting Entities

It was noted above that the legal-entity status of the
incorporated business enterprise led naturally to its position
as an accounting entity. One may nonetheless harbor reserva-
tions about any automatic tie between status as a legal entity and status as an accounting entity.

A legal entity does not _per se_ connote an accounting

---

[1] Henry Rand Hatfield, "An Historical Defence of Bookkeeping," in W. T. Baxter (editor), Studies in Accounting
(London: Sweet & Maxwell, Limited, 1950), pp. 1-12, at p. 11.

entity, and an accounting entity does not per se connote a legal entity. Accounting[1] is concerned with economic units --whether they are legal units or not. Accounting endeavors to measure the impact on the business enterprise of various economic phenomena. Insofar as events of economic signifi- cance also carry legal implications, the latter are valid raw material for accounting recognition. To be sure, the creation of a legal unit may additionally be the creation of an economic unit--if the legal unit is to be the locus of profit-seeking economic activity. Existence of a legal unit alone, however, is not enough, for it is not the purpose of accounting to trace solely the legal rights and duties of the legal unit.[2]

Factors other than legislative enabling acts have served to imbue the incorporated firm with accounting-entity status. The increased size and complexity of many corpora- tions by the end of the nineteenth century contributed to the notion that such an aggregation of capital is a locus of economic activity in its own right and not merely an offshoot of the owner's personality. This belief was strengthened by the broad gulf between corporate ownership and corporate man-

---

[1]By "accounting" is meant financial accounting, or the systematic development of accounting data for external finan- cial statements.

[2]Although the occurrence of a purely legal event may be used as a criterion for making an accounting decision (for example, looking to the legal passage of title in order to recognize revenue), the legal event is used presumably only because it affords objective evidence of a real change in the economic status of the parties concerned.

agement which--at least in the United States--began to appear
in the last decade of the nineteenth century. Moreover, an
important principle ingrained in the first U. S. income tax
law was that a corporation, being a legal entity, is an entity for tax purposes.[1] This collection of legal, economic,
and political developments effectively placed corporations,
for accounting purposes, beyond the reach of the proprietary
postulate.

If the firm is to be accorded status as an accounting
entity, Paciolo's capital account (for a corporation) would
assume the character of a kind of liability,[2] rather than
that of a conduit to the owner's personality. As Schumpeter
observes:

> The only realistic definition of stockholders is
> that they are creditors (capitalists) who forego
> part of the legal protection usually extended to
> creditors, in exchange for the right to partici-
> pate in profits. To the economist, the legal con-
> struction of an equity in this case is but a law-
> yer's fiction that almost caricatures the real
> situation.[3]

But one should not--at this point--generalize the
application of the accounting entity as to all firms. Here
the discussion applies only to the incorporated enterprise.

---

[1]See Goode, op. cit., p. 9.

[2]It is a "kind of liability" rather than a liability
in the usual sense--that is, having a due date. Viewed as a
"kind of liability," the proprietorship is a continuing and
ultimate obligation of the firm to its owners.

[3]Joseph A. Schumpeter, Business Cycles: A Theoretical,
Historical, and Statistical Analysis of the Capitalist Process
(New York: McGraw-Hill Book Company, Inc., 1939), I: p. 104;
emphasis supplied.

Accounting at the Turn of the Century -
A Review

The changing nature of the mainstream of business activity--that is, toward relative permanence of the firm-- suggested to accountants that the assumption of "continuity" of operations should replace that of the "venture."[1] The growth of the corporate form of enterprise caused the gradual acceptance of the entity postulate as being more consistent with the character of corporate activity. Due either to statutory requirement or to the managers' demonstrated need for periodic financial reports, accountants adopted a rule of "periodicity." Income and capital were to be kept separate, and the profit figure attained new prominence. The method of periodically valuing net worth (as might have been justifiable for medieval times) proved to be too haphazard and subjective (that is, indefensible in the face of alternative reasonable valuations) for modern, continuous business enterprise--if it was not too haphazard and subjective in medieval times as well. Although the market-value method has had its stanch advocates in the last fifty years,[2] the more

---

[1] Under the heading, "Principle in Valuation of Assets," Dicksee writes in 1900: "It being the primary object of most ordinary undertakings to continue to carry on operations, it is but fair that the assets enumerated in a Balance Sheet be valued with that end in view. . . ." Lawrence R. Dicksee, Auditing: A Practical Manual for Auditors (4th ed.: London: Gee & Co., 1900), p. 159.

[2] Among those are DR Scott, Theory of Accounts (2 vols.; New York: Henry Holt and Company, 1925), Vol. I; and (more vituperative) Kenneth MacNeal, Truth in Accounting (Philadelphia: University of Pennsylvania Press, 1939). Of the more recent advocates is R. J. Chambers. See his "Measurement and Misrepresentation," in Management Science, VI, No. 2 (January, 1960), pp. 141-48.

objective approach of acquisition cost ("historical cost")
has prevailed.

Raison D'être of the Matching Concept

For the final floor board underneath the profit-
determination process, accountants seized upon the period in
which the sale occurs as the period in which the causally-
expired costs (that is, asset values) should be recognized--
and labeled "expenses." The axis about which the cost factors were to rotate was the revenues: when the sale was con-
summated (usually deemed to occur at the time of delivery),
the related cost expiration would be restated as expenses.
Revenues less expenses (ignoring for the time being losses,
income taxes, and interest charges) yielded profit, or net
income. The selection of revenues as the commanding element
was not merely an arbitrary decision. As indicated above,
accountants looked askance at a premature recognition of
profit--that is, before the sale was binding and (in most
cases) final. Mere conjecture, often tied to a hitching post
of business optimism, would not suffice. The acquisition of
merchandise alone does not (in the normal course) insure its
sale. Hence, the so-called "matching process," or the matching of costs with related revenues, grew up in a climate of
objectivity and certainty.[1]

---

[1]See Changing Concepts, p. 28; and W. A. Paton and
A. C. Littleton, An Introduction to Corporate Accounting
Standards (Chicago: American Accounting Association, 1940),
Monograph No. 3, chap. 2, especially pp. 18-21.

But does the matching process produce a net income which is in agreement with the economist's concept? Is not a man's income, as Hicks avers, "the maximum value which he can consume during a week, and still expect to be as well off at the end of the week as he was at the beginning"?[1] "We may define the income of a corporation in a given year," writes Alexander, "as the amount the corporation can distribute to the owners of equity in the corporation and be as well off at the end of the year as at the beginning."[2]

If these definitions of income (or net income) are accepted as valid, why cannot the Venetian annual valuation approach be adapted to the modern corporation? An answer is proferred by May:

> In an earlier age, when capital assets were inconsiderable and business units in general smaller and less complex than they are today, it was possible to value assets with comparative ease and accuracy and to measure the progress made from year to year by annual valuations. With the growing mechanization of industry, and with corporate organizations becoming constantly larger, more completely integrated and more complex, this has become increasingly impractic-

---

[1] J. R. Hicks, Value and Capital (London: Oxford University Press, 1946), Second Edition, p. 172.

[2] Sidney S. Alexander, "Income Measurement in a Dynamic Economy," in Study Group on Business Income: Five Monographs (New York: American Institute of Accountants, 1950), pp. 1-95, at p. 15.
And Marshall: "When a man is engaged in business, his profits for the year are the excess of his receipts from his business during the year over his outlay for his business. The difference between the value of his stock of plant, material, etc. at the end and at the beginning of the year is taken as part of his receipts or as part of his outlay, according as there has been an increase or decrease of value." Alfred Marshall, Principles of Economics (8th ed.; New York: The Macmillan Company, 1948 [originally published in 1920]), p. 74.

able. From an accounting standpoint, the distinguishing characteristic of business today is the extent to
which expenditures are made in one period with the
definite purpose and expectation that they shall be
the means of producing profits in the future; and how
such expenditures shall be dealt with in accounts is
the central problem of financial accounting. How much
of a given expenditure of the current or a past year
shall be carried forward as an asset can not possibly
be determined by an exercise of judgment in the nature
of a valuation. The task of appraisal would be too
vast, and the variations in appraisal from year to
year due to changes in price levels or changes in the
mental attitude of the appraisers would in many cases
be so great as to reduce all other elements in the
computations of the results of operations to relative
insignificance.
Carrying the thought one stage further, it is
apparent that the real value of the assets of any
large business is dependent mainly on the earning
capacity of the enterprise. This fact is fairly generally recognized by intelligent investors as regards
capital assets such as plant and machinery, but it is
not equally generally recognized that it is true,
though to a lesser extent, in respect of such assets
as inventories and trade accounts receivable. Those,
however, who have had experience in liquidations and
reorganizations realize that in many industries it
becomes impossible to realize inventories or accounts
receivable at more than a fraction of their going-
concern value, once the business has ceased to be a
going concern. To attempt to arrive at the value of
the assets of a business annually by an estimation of
the earning capacity of the enterprise would be an impossible and unprofitable task. Any consideration of
the accounts of a large business enterprise of today
must start from the premise that an annual valuation
of the assets is neither practical nor desirable.[1]

Although he does not use the word specifically in the above

quotation, May clearly refers to the hazards of <u>uncertainty</u>.

---

[1]George O. May, in a letter of September 22, 1932 to
the Committee on Stock List, New York Stock Exchange, reproduced in <u>Audits of Corporate Accounts</u>, Correspondence between
the Special Committee on Co-operation with Stock Exchanges
of the American Institute of Accountants and the Committee
on Stock List of the New York Stock Exchange, 1932-1934
([n.p.:] American Institute of Accountants, 1934), pp. 5-7.

Elsewhere it has been argued that even with certainty of the
magnitude of the future cash flows and their time distribution, the question of the interest rate remains a subjective
matter.[1]

Boulding defines the profit or loss of a discrete
investment as the difference between revenue and outlay.[2]
For a single, separate investment, this criterion would not
only be correct but workable. Storey succinctly demonstrates
that, for the typical business enterprise today, Boulding's
criterion is infeasible:

> The problem of accounting is not . . . the simple
> measurement of the difference between total revenue
> and total outlay over the life of an investment, but
> that of measuring the difference between revenues and
> expenses for a given segment of that life. Modern
> accounting breaks up a continuous stream of business
> activity into artificial segments known as accounting
> periods. This operation is designated as periodic
> income determination.
> This problem of periodic income determination is
> inseparably connected with that of property valuation.
> . . .[3]

. . . .

---

[1]Even if the future cash flows and their time distributions are known with certainty, what interest rate should
be used? The prevailing rate for a particular kind of loan?
The earning rate of the firm during the past year? during the
past several years? how many? Even if a rate is selected,
what if it changes? In determining the present value of a
"plant asset" a year after its acquisition, should one use
the rate which was used a year earlier or the rate as it
stands today? For further discussion on this point, see Alexander, "Income Measurement in a Dynamic Economy," in Study
Group, especially p. 26.

[2]Kenneth E. Boulding, Economic Analysis (New York:
Harper & Brothers, 1955), Third Edition, pp. 840-41.

[3]Reed K. Storey, "Cash Movements and Periodic Income
Determination," The Accounting Review, XXXV, No. 3 (July,
1960), 449-54, at p. 450.

[The value of an asset is] equal to the discounted
value of the future net receipts from the asset, discounted at the profit rate.[1]
The most serious problems encountered in the measurement of periodic net profit are the result of
man's inability to foretell the future accurately.
Inasmuch as the results of business decisions cannot
be known, periodic income can only be estimated until
such time as the effects of the decisions have all become apparent. . . .

. . . .

The accountant's reaction to this uncertainty . . .
is to rely on accounting principles and conventions,
especially those relating to the use of objective evidence as a basis for estimates, consistent treatment of
items, and full disclosure of circumstances.[2]

Clearly, uncertainty about the future precludes the

ascertainment of a true value for the assets (and, conjointly,

a true net income) of a continuing concern--except at the term-

ination of the enterprise.[3] As Hicks points out, the firm's

optimal production plan is found by measuring the present

value of the excesses of the future receipts over future out-

lays as a result of employing the firm's resources in all al-

ternative lines of endeavor.[4] The present value of the firm's

assets, it follows, is derived from an analysis of the re-

ceipts and disbursements in connection with which the assets

are to be employed. The amounts and time-distributions of

these future flows being uncertain, it is impossible to ac-

complish precisely the task with which the accountant is

charged. As an approximation technique, therefore, account-

---

[1] Ibid., p. 451.   [2] Ibid., p. 452.

[3] At this juncture, evidently, no future receipts
need to be considered.

[4] Hicks, op. cit., chap. 15 generally, especially pp.
196-97.

ants have selected an accounting process which embodies the "matching concept."

Written Evidence of the Development of Nineteenth-Century Accounting Thought

The preceding discussion considers the significant economic, political, and social developments since the seventeenth century and their apparent impact on the nature of the accounting process. In contrast, it will be instructive to survey the evolution of accounting thought in nineteenth-century writings. Although Littleton cites that 100-year period as "the formative period of accountancy,"[1] one finds scant evidence of adolescent behavior in the written words of those years. As will be shown, the general trend of nineteenth-century accounting thought is not unlike that of the two or three preceding centuries. More appropriately, one might choose the 50-year period from 1875 to 1925 as the "formative years," for during this interval the revision of the accounting process (so as to be in harmony with the entity postulate and other newly appropriate assumptions and rules) appears to have achieved crystallization in accounting literature.[2]

F. W. Cronhelm, writing in 1818, espouses the pro-

---

[1]Littleton, Evolution, p. 165.

[2]Paton's magnum opus, in this writer's view, was the climactic work of this period. It was the crystallization, the comprehensive and critical treatise in accounting theory. William Andrew Paton, Accounting Theory--With Special Reference to the Corporate Enterprise (New York: The Ronald Press Company, 1922).

prietary view: "The purpose of Book-keeping, as a record of property, is to shew the owner at all times the value of his whole capital, and of every part of it."[1] His fundamental bookkeeping equation is

Positive Property - Negative Property = Stock;

he stressed the equivalence of capital with its constituent parts (that is, properties).[2]

As to the place of the nominal accounts and profit determination, Cronhelm states:

> The Accounts of Profit and Loss are simply branches of the Stock, their object being to prevent numerous petty entries in the latter, to collect together the individual augmentations and diminutions of the capital, and to transfer the general result in one entry to the Stock. In like manner, Commission, Interest, &c., are merely ramifications of the Profit and Loss Accounts, which prevent numerous petty entries in the latter, collect the aggregates of their respective departments, and transfer the results in one branch from the Stock, its use being to record all sums put into the business or withdrawn, so as to keep them entirely distinct from the Profit and Loss. The result of the Private Account is also transferred in one entry to the Stock.[3]

Rather than having conceptual significance in itself, profit was merely the boiled-down "augmentations and diminutions of the capital"--almost a procedural expedient.

Thomas Jones, an American who wrote in 1841 and 1859,[4] was among the first to recognize in print that the set of nom-

---

[1] Quoted in Littleton, Evolution, p. 168.

[2] Ibid.   [3] Ibid., p. 169.

[4] Not to be confused with Edward Thomas Jones, an Englishman who wrote at the turn of the nineteenth century. Edward Thomas Jones is quoted above, Chapter II, p. 39.

inal accounts was a necessary <u>theoretical</u> part of the accounting schemata. He placed the balance sheet and the profit and loss statement on the same plane of importance.
Double-entry, he writes "embraces two distinct plans of ar-
ranging the facts--each plan involving a distinct set of
accounts."[1] He states that it is "our general object . . .
to compare the decrease or outgoing with the increase or in-
coming; and although a sum expended is not always literally
a loss, it has the same effect of decreasing our means, and
vice versa with gains."[2]

Jones, according to Littleton, represents a break
from the centuries of emphasis on the personification of
accounts.[3] To virtually all earlier writers, the real (or
personal) accounts were the only ones of significance to the
determination of the firm's success. Nominal accounts, previously being only procedural niceties, were to rank <u>pari
passu</u> with the real accounts.

Other nineteenth-century writers, including Kurzbauer,

---

[1]Quoted in Littleton, <u>Evolution</u>, p. 172.

[2]<u>Ibid.</u>, p. 176.

[3]By "personification of accounts" is meant the practice of accounting writers of ascribing a personality to the
"real" accounts and saying, for example, "Inventory received
$xxx from Plant and Equipment; debit the receiver, credit the
giver." In this manner, the accounting student is encouraged
to think of the process of debiting and crediting accounts as
being illustrative of dealings between persons. Cole followed
this practice as recently as 1915. William Morse Cole,
<u>Accounts--Their Construction and Interpretation</u> (rev. and enl.
ed.; Boston: Houghton Mifflin Company, 1915).

testified to the importance of <u>two</u> sets of accounts; however, they were a minority.[1] Bookkeeping texts of that century by and large adhered to the older, personification approach. In this connection, it is interesting to note that the economic, political, and social phenomena which were to revolutionize the accounting process had little impact on nineteenth-century accounting and bookkeeping literature.

A few nineteenth-century writers appear to have favored an entity view of the business enterprise. Berliner, a German writer, in 1887 advocated the separation of business capital from the owner's private property. He maintained that commercial bookkeeping was only a mirror of this separately dedicated capital. He viewed business assets as debts of the firm to the proprietor and business liabilities as claims of the firm against the proprietor.[2]

At this time, German accounting writers, as well as

---

[1] See Littleton, Evolution, p. 180.

[2] Berliner's interpretation, here paraphrased, of the true nature of business liabilities is disturbing. Even in the face of his interpretation of the true nature of business assets (which interpretation, by itself, would suggest at least a first approximation of the entity view), his statement as to business liabilities leads one to believe that Berliner saw the firm as only a conduit for the owner and parties who dealt with the firm. Evidently, Berliner viewed the owner as more than a kind of "third-party beneficiary" of the firm. Indeed, Berliner's firm appears to be an agent of Berliner's owner, the principal--all of which is reminiscent of the Roman slave's accounting and "agency accounting" in general. For a discussion of the Roman slave's accounting, see above, Chapter II, pp. 13-14, and this chapter, pp. 51-52. Berliner's analysis anticipates the static model of Canning and the position of Husband. See the relevant sections of Chapter V.

E. G. Folsom, an American, began to relate cost and return, effort and effect--in contrast to a "real" or balance-sheet analysis. Indeed, their terminology was loose, for example, interchanging loss and expense as though they were identical concepts. Still, the center of attention was turned to other than just ownership-and-debt considerations.[1]

Notwithstanding these occasional entity-oriented excursions, the mainstream of nineteenth-century accounting and bookkeeping writings continued to embody the proprietary view.

Concluding Observations

We have thus noted the existence of two rather divergent views of the business enterprise (each apparently in harmony with particular economic facts)--the proprietary and entity approaches. Neither approach, however, explains anything. Neither is a theory. On the contrary, each is an assumption as to the manner in which the business enterprise should be conceived. Like other assumptions or postulates, each may influence the body of principle which is built thereupon.

This chapter has attempted to sort out the alteration of one postulate (that is, the orientation postulate) from the repercussions thereof on other postulates and on rules and principles derived thereupon. In this way, it is hoped that one could appreciate that a postulate is not a theory in itself but only a line of approach to a theory.

---

[1] Littleton, _Evolution_, pp. 195-203.

CHAPTER IV

THE PROPRIETARY AND ENTITY VIEWS EXAMINED

The purpose of this chapter is to analyze the meaning and implications for accounting theory of the proprietary
and entity views--two interpretations of the orientation postulate. The contents of Chapters II and III, as historical
surveys of the somewhat parallel development of politico-
economic institutions and accounting theory, provide the
necessary backdrop and frame of reference for the present
chapter.

At the outset, a reclassification of the several versions of the orientation postulate is essayed in order to
clarify the differences between each view. The principal
features of the two major opposing views are then subjected
to critical examination for the purpose of assaying the true
accounting import of each. Finally, Paton's Accounting Theory,
which contains the first significant presentation and defense
of the entity view, is accorded critical attention.

A Re-examination of the Multiple Phases of the Orientation Postulate

A statement of the point of view that the accounting
process ought to assume, the orientation postulate, as will
be shown, is divisible into two largely independent questions.

First, should the accounting unit--that is, the locus

of economic activities that are the subject matter of the
accounting process--be the owner or the enterprise (or some
other economic body)? Second, should the results of the
unit's economic activity be aimed at the owner or should they
be directed at all capital suppliers (or at another party or
parties)?[1] These questions relate to the first and second
"subpostulate," respectively. Among the several possibilities are the following: the view (first subpostulate) that
the owner is the proper unit for which the accounting is to
be made (and, implicitly, that the owner is the party to whom
the accounting results are to be directed); the view (first
subpostulate) that the enterprise is the proper unit for
which the accounting is to be made, together with the view
(second subpostulate) that the accounting results are to be
aimed at the owner; and the view (first subpostulate) that
the enterprise is the proper unit for which the accounting
is to be made, together with the view (second subpostulate)
that the accounting results are to be directed toward all
capital suppliers. The first subpostulate seeks a determination of the economic organism for which an accounting is to

---

[1]Except where otherwise indicated, income (= net income, profit, or profits) will refer to the capital suppliers
on whose capital the income is a return. Such phraseology as
"return to the entity" will be avoided, for it is this writer's
view that, whether or not the enterprise is treated as the
accounting unit, income should be viewed as an equitable interest on the part of some or all capital suppliers in the
assets of the firm. Regardless of how rigorously one wishes
to interpret the enterprise as the accounting unit, it should
not be forgotten that the ultimate beneficiaries of economic
activity--as participants in the productive process or as
consumers--are individuals.

be effected. The second subpostulate seeks a determination
of the party (or parties) to whom the accounting results for
that economic organism are to be aimed. Both subpostulates
deal with the orientation of the accounting process.

In the light of this more precise delineation of the
subdivisions of the orientation postulate, a revised terminology is in order. The principal, or unit, which is chosen
under the first subpostulate will be termed "the subject."
The principal, or party, to whom the results are to be aimed
will be termed "the beneficiary." The medieval merchant,
for purposes of this set of shorthand expressions, will be
termed "economic citizen" (to borrow a phrase from Paton).[1]
Through the accounting merger of his business and personal
affairs he was unquestionably the focal point of the accounting process. This situation is expressed by the designation
"economic-citizen-subject." He was also the beneficiary of
the accounting data.

Subsequent to the time when accountants had decided
to separate business from personal affairs, the owner was
still the central figure, but as a proprietor rather than as
an "economic citizen." The representation of these facts in
the first subpostulate will be "proprietor-subject." He
again, it is assumed, was the beneficiary of the accounting
results.

---

[1]William Andrew Paton, Accounting Theory--With Special Reference to the Corporate Enterprise (New York: The
Ronald Press Company, 1922), p. 63.

To those who would characterize the enterprise as a separate, accountable entity, the term "entity-subject" will be appropriate. If the beneficiary of the data is to be all capital suppliers, the designation "equities-beneficiary" will represent the second subpostulate. "Proprietor-beneficiary" will stand for the view that only the residual equity holders are to be the object of the accounting process.

Graphically, the relationships might be as follows:

FIRST SUBPOSTULATE		SECOND SUBPOSTULATE[1]
economic-citizen-subject	&	[economic-citizen-beneficiary]
proprietor-subject	&	[proprietor-beneficiary]
entity-subject	&	proprietor-beneficiary
entity-subject	&	equities-beneficiary

In this study, "equity holders" and "capital suppliers" will be used interchangeably. "Equities," employed here in the Patonian sense, comprehend the conventional categories of "liabilities and capital," that is, the interests that are customarily represented on the right-hand side of the balance sheet. But Paton does not associate net income with _all_ capital suppliers.[2]

---

[1]The use of brackets in the tabular presentation indicates that the bracketed subpostulate is implied by articulation only of its accompanying (that is, the "first") subpostulate. Mention of a subpostulate with the intent of implying its accompanying subpostulate will usually be indicated by using the word "postulate" rather than merely "subpostulate."

[2]Paton, _op. cit._, pp. 37-43, 68-75. Writes Paton: "Current liabilities that arise as a result of the purchase of commodities and services 'on time' . . . represent equities, but not income-bearing interests." He adds: "Evidently, then, [net income] may be defined essentially from the standpoint of the relatively long-term, capital-furnishing, income-bearing equities." _Ibid._, p. 264; see related discussion on pp. 260-64, _ibid._ Cf. Paton's more recent discussion of the "all-capital earning rate," in William A. Paton and Robert L. Dixon,

The Implications for Accounting Theory of the Ascendancy of Proprietor-Subject, Going-Concern, and Periodicity Postulates[1]

It was noted in the previous chapter that the current-price conception of the all-important asset-valuation process was displaced by the cost principle. The matching concept was a natural consequence of this change. To what extent was this reformulation brought about by the new version of the orientation postulate, that is, from economic-citizen-subject to proprietor-subject? What factors appear to have been instrumental in calling forth this new approach to asset valuation?

As noted above, essentially the same commercial revolution which urged the separation of business from personal affairs also demonstrated the worthiness of the continuity, or going-concern, postulate. At about the same time, as already pointed out, a need for periodicity in accounting reports became manifest. It is here submitted that together these alterations in the foundation of postulates caused the aforementioned restructuring of the overlay of principle. It is further submitted that the increasing validity of the

_____

Essentials of Accounting (New York: The Macmillan Company, 1958), pp. 750-55.
        See also footnote 2, p. 130, and footnote 1, pp. 192-93, infra.

[2] As pointed out in footnote 1, p. 98, "Proprietor-Subject" implies the entire postulate, "proprietor-subject, proprietor-beneficiary." Consistent with footnote 2, p. 47, of Chapter III, the term "postulate" will be understood to include "rule."

going-concern assumption was far more powerful a force in this respect than was the restated orientation postulate.

It will be recalled that--to a significant extent--commercial undertakings of the economic-citizen-subject medieval period were sporadic and had a tenuous existence. An assumption of continuity for the typical enterprise of that day probably would have been unsupportable. Generally ignoring income-statement-type data, the medieval merchant was interested almost exclusively in the changes in his net worth.[1] In this setting, it would not have been incongruous to ascertain periodic net worth by employing current market valuations,[2] even of the net worth directly (instead of dealing with the assets and liabilities) were there a valid means of making a market test of such ownership interests. To be sure, the relatively simple asset structures, that is, mostly short-lived resources, lent themselves to a comparatively easy market testing of their values.

But the emergence of the continuity assumption, together with demands of the periodicity postulate, effectively

---

[1] It will be noted that the term "net worth," commonly employed in accounting expositions that stress the pre-eminence of proprietorship, implies an economic or market valuation.

[2] It should be carefully noted that the words "current prices" and "current values," or their singular forms, denote the market prices at the present time for the assets so described. Only the term "present values," or its singular form, will be used in this study to denote the actuarial calculation of the value at the moment of the time-adjusted future net receipts scheduled to result from the utilization by the enterprise of its cost factors (i. e., inventories, plant assets, and the like).

forced a corresponding adjustment in accounting principles.
No longer was the life of the enterprise thought to be relatively short; an enterprise was assumed to be a going concern. Asset values, it follows, could no longer be judged
according to direct[1] market criteria; they derived their
economic significance from the (estimated) magnitude of their
contributions to the future enhancement (that is, net receipts)
of the enterprise. Theirs was a value in use, not a value in
exchange.

The periodicity postulate, moreover, fostered the demand that net-worth readings be taken at arbitrary intervals
notwithstanding the inherent uncertainty of the internally-
derived asset values.

Market values, by definition, would not serve as values in use.[2] Recourse had to be made to the economic sur-
roundings within which the assets were to become effective
resources--and, by assumption, they were to be devoted to
employment within a continuing enterprise. Indeed, the in-

---

[1]By "direct" is meant valuation of extant assets by
reference to markets where those assets are traded. Going-
concern valuations inevitably use market tests--but they are
tests, taken at various times in the future, of the salable
product or service of the enterprise. In this sense, the
valuations are described as "indirect."

[2]This statement is true of cost factors only (see
footnote 2, p. 100, for some examples of cost factors).
Cash and claims to cash--assets that may be used to purchase
the cost factors that, in turn, may be converted into products or services that will be desired by customers--derive
their value to the firm via the current prices that are attached to them in the marketplace. The cost factors, however, derive their value to the firm via the future net receipts that accrue to the firm at the time of sale (or at
another appropriate time at which revenues are recognized
in the books).

creasingly complex, long-term asset structures--to the ac-
companiment of a changing technology which has acted to render many existing assets obsolete--largely defies valuation
by market test.

As a result of theoretical and practical necessity,
therefore, the medieval "current valuation approach," so
serviceable in the light of the facts of that day, had to be
rejected for the kind of enterprise that began to appear in
the latter stages of the nineteenth century. And as will be
shown below, a significant number of twentieth-century accounting writers acknowledged the appropriateness of the
going-concern assumption.[1]

Almost lost in this chain reaction from changes in
postulates to changes in principles is the roughly concurrent

---

[1]The advent of the separation of owners from the day-
to-day operation of the enterprise, causing the emergence of
a class of professional managers, suggests the necessity of
what might be called the "accountability postulate." By its
terms, financial reports should reflect the managers' account
of the efficacy of their decisions. In this regard, the in-
currence of cost results from a managerial decision. Current
market prices fluctuate beyond the control, as a rule, of any
company of managers. Consequently, the financial reports of
accounting units in which managers are not also the owners
should use cost, not current prices, for measuring the dollar
amount of the assets for which the managers are accountable.
As a result of evolving forms of economic organization, therefore, both the ascendancy of the "going concern"
and "accountability" assumptions jointly can be used to enable the superstructure of principles and concepts to include
the emphasis on cost. It should be noted, however, that
"cost" is "historical cost"--as expressed in dollars of uniform purchasing power. In this respect, this writer is in
full agreement with Paton. See William A. Paton and William
A. Paton, Jr., Corporation Accounts and Statements (New York:
The Macmillan Company, 1955), chap. 19.

separation of business from personal affairs: the ascendancy of the new version of the orientation postulate. Ironically perhaps, the revision of this postulate appears to have had only an ancillary influence on the restatement of the overlay of principle. In itself, the division of personal and business affairs would not seem to cause the overturn of the value-in-exchange approach, although it would assist the owner in evaluating the purely commercial aspects of his various activities. In this latter respect, the alteration of the orientation postulate contributed to the theoretical (and practical) efficacy of the value-in-use principle. Specifically, it prevented the household and other commercial affairs of the owner from obfuscating the economic outlines of the enterprise in question. The alteration in the orientation postulate was no more potent than this; it was a contributing factor, but alone it would have accomplished little.

Hence, at a time when the notion of separateness of the firm received a large measure of credence in accounting circles, other developments were more forceful in bringing about a revision of accounting principle. What was in fact a kind of correlation among several factors working at about the same time should not be interpreted as causality. That the new version of the orientation postulate was a contributing factor cannot be denied. That it was the cause, or even a major cause, of the restatement of principle must be rejected. There was nothing in the new orientation postu-

late[1] _per se_ that required a change in the principles of valuation; what it _did_ accomplish was the restriction of the
valuation process to only enterprise-related assets.

A Critical Evaluation of the Proprietary and Entity Views

The different conceptions of the orientation postulate require careful delineation from each other in order
that their respective implications for the superstructure of
accounting principles and concepts might be studied.

Medievals, as already observed, established the individual merchant as the undisputed center of accounting attention. He was The Economic Citizen. No serious attempt
at separating his business affairs from personal transactions
appears to have been made. The accounting structure was
erected about the merchant as an individual. Hence, this
conception was described above, in the shorthand of this
study, as the economic-citizen-subject postulate; the accounting report being rendered for (and by) the individual himself,
there is no purpose to be served by labeling the economic
citizen as the "beneficiary" also of the data.

The economic developments surveyed in Chapter II,
chiefly the evolution of capitalistic enterprise, seem to
have been instrumental in redirecting emphasis from the merchant as an economic citizen to (at the least) the merchant

---

[1]This statement is true whether one adopts the proprietor-subject postulate or the entity-subject, proprietor-
beneficiary postulate--both being interpretations of the orientation postulate.

in his purely capitalistic, or enterprise, capacity. The
departure, in relative terms, of the venture or caravan type
of commercial endeavor appears also largely responsible for
the ascendancy of the going-concern postulate. And by the
conclusion of the nineteenth century, it was evident in the
United States as well as in England that accountants had come
to favor the separation, for accounting purposes, of business
affairs from personal affairs.[1]

But this division in itself did not imply also an
entire shift of emphasis from the individual to the firm.
The central figure, as Gilman recounts,[2] was still to be the
individual--but more specifically in his role as proprietor
of the firm. He was seen as owning the firm's assets and
owing its liabilities; the firm was not viewed as a full-
fledged entity in its own right, but as a unit only to the
extent that it was necessary to segregate under its aegis the
separately-dedicated proprietary properties. Beyond that,
the firm was interpreted only as a means to an end, a sort
of conduit through which a measure of the increase or decrease
in the proprietor's "net wealth"[3] could be ascertained. The
accounting for changes in proprietorship remained as important

[1]For authority, the reader might consult any of the
numerous books that were written between 1890 and 1915, some
of which are cited below in this chapter.

[2]Stephen Gilman, Accounting Concepts of Profit (New
York: The Ronald Press Company, 1939), p. 48.

[3]"Net wealth" is a favorite phrase of Hatfield. See,
for example, Henry Rand Hatfield, Modern Accounting--Its
Principles and Some of Its Problems (New York: D. Appleton
and Company, 1909), p. 14.

as it was to medievals, but instead it referred only to properties devoted to the enterprise. This interpretation of
the firm-proprietor relationship may be called the proprietor-subject postulate, the proprietor once again being
assumed to be the party to whom the accounting results were
addressed.

With the further development of the modern corporation,[1] came another shift in emphasis: the business enterprise rather than its owner became the center of accounting
attention. The business assumed the role of a self-contained
accounting entity, reporting to either some or all of its
capital suppliers. Accounting writers label their conception
of the second stage of development in the orientation postulate as the "proprietary theory,"[2] and the third stage as the
"entity theory."

In recent years, these writers have frequently assayed
the merits of each of these two views in an endeavor to select
the one most appropriate for use. It is this writer's contention that many of these writers have misrepresented the

---

[1]For an authoritative discussion of this development,
see Adolph A. Berle, Jr. and Gardiner C. Means, The Modern
Corporation and Private Property (New York: Commerce Clearing
House, Inc., 1932).

[2]As pointed out in Chapter III, the different views
of the orientation postulate are not principles, concepts, or
theories. Because most of the writers quoted below nonetheless refer to these views as principles, concepts, or theories, this terminology will be largely retained in this chapter. Quotation marks, however, will be used to distinguish
the terminology of these authors from the more nearly correct terminology.

true difference between (1) the views themselves, and (2) the ramifications upon accounting theory of each view. Because of the nature of these distortions, one of the alternatives--the "proprietary theory"--has been erroneously advanced as a valid candidate. It is here contended that the real choice today (in terms of either the "proprietary theory" or the "entity theory" or both), as well as during the last several decades, is and has been between two versions of the "entity theory." In the language of the above reclassification, they are the proprietor-beneficiary and equities-beneficiary versions of the postulate that has as its first subdivision the entity-subject view.

At the outset, it should be iterated that accountants generally agree that economic rather than legal factors are determinative of the choice of a point of view.[1] It follows that the choice of a point of view would apply to a given case regardless of the legal status of the business enterprise involved, except insofar as its economic nature is dictated by its legal nature.[2]

---

[1]See, for example, Walter Gerry Kell, "The Equities Concept and Its Application to Accounting Theory" (unpublished Ph.D. dissertation, Graduate College, University of Illinois, 1952), pp. 24-25, 27-28, and 194; and W. A. Paton and A. C. Littleton, An Introduction to Corporate Accounting Standards (Chicago: American Accounting Association, 1940), Monograph No. 3, pp. 8-9.

[2]This does not suggest that one point of view should, as a kind of categorical imperative, be applicable to every form of business organization, but that it should be applicable only to those enterprises that qualify due to the context of their economic settings--regardless of what legal forms those enterprises may have. Depending on the economic nature of a given enterprise, irrespective of purely legal considerations, one of several possible "points of view" should be applied.

The argument is best begun by the observation that it is difficult to be certain whether many writers of note ever did advocate the "proprietary theory." Sprague, Hatfield, and Kester are the most commonly-mentioned names in connection with this "theory."[1] But there is reason to believe that even they were not convinced of its validity for accounting purposes. It can at least be shown that their adherence to its doctrines (that is, insofar as a postulate can be said to have "doctrines") is at times inconstant; occasionally their words gainsay their presumed loyalty to its holdings. And there is no question that their notions of its implications for accounting theory are at odds with those that are itemized by the recent comparers of the two "theories."

As to Sprague,[2] it can be argued that he employed the "proprietary theory" only as a pedagogical device, in order to engage the reader's interest in the illustrated situation and, consequently, his interest in the subject matter. In his first four chapters, but to a noticeably lesser extent in the remaining exposition, Sprague uses the pronouns "we," "I," "me," "my," and "our," among others, to humanize the proprietorship examples. With these words, he effectively communicates to the reader the "proprietary-theory"

---

[1]See, for example, Gilman, op. cit., p. 50; Paton, Theory, pp. iii, 51-52; and A. C. Littleton, Accounting Evolution to 1900 (New York: American Institute Publishing Co., Inc., 1933), p. 184.

[2]Charles E. Sprague, The Philosophy of Accounts (New York: Charles E. Sprague, 1907).

notion that the proprietor owns the business assets and owes the business liabilities. Other statements, however, seem to belie his presumed attachment to the "proprietary theory." After having transformed his proprietorship example into one for a partnership, Sprague observes, "A new business entity has been created distinct from Jones and from Smith; it is a collectiv [sic] unity but a real one."[1] He also refers to the corporation as a "business entity . . . but still personal and real."[2] If it is contended that he means to say here only that a corporation is a <u>legal</u> entity, which is true, it may be argued in opposition that his statement that the proprietor owns the assets and owes the liabilities of the proprietorship is also nothing more than a <u>legal</u> truth. Into which statement does Sprague want to breathe a modicum of <u>accounting</u> substance? Which is the proper <u>accounting</u> view-- without regard to solely legal considerations of the business enterprise?

If Sprague did not embrace the "proprietary theory," one might contend, why did he dissent from Irving Fisher's conception of the firm as a "fictitious person"? It is true that Sprague disagreed with Fisher in this general area, but it seems that Sprague's reaction was not against Fisher's

---

[1] Ibid., p. 33. Sprague, it can be seen from his spelling of "collective," was desirous of eliminating from English spellings the "superfluous," or unpronounced, letters. Hence, his printings of <u>The Philosophy of Accounts</u> contain a number of unconventional spellings. See, for example, the extracts that appear on the following few pages.

[2] Ibid., p. 35.

"fictitious person" as such. Fisher writes:

> It is well to note here the distinction between
> the accounting of real persons and of fictitious
> persons. For a real person, the assets may be and
> usually are in excess of the liabilities, and the
> difference is the capital-balance of that person.
> This capital is not to be regarded as a liability,
> but as a balance or difference between the liabil-
> ities and the assets. For a fictitious person, on
> the other hand, as for instance a corporation or a
> partnership [sic!], the liabilities are always ex-
> actly equal to the assets; for the balancing item
> called capital is as truly an obligation from the
> fictitious person to the real stockholders, as any
> of the other liabilities. A fictitious person, in
> fact, is a mere bookkeeping dummy, holding certain
> assets and owing all of them out again to real per-
> sons.[1]

Disagreeing with Fisher, Sprague argues:

> In this I think [Fisher] has been misled by the
> lazy habit of bookkeepers in calling all the credit
> balances liabilities, altho they know that some of
> those balances are not liabilities. Even admitting
> that there is a fictitious entity it owes nothing to
> the real owners. It merely is a composit ownership
> which again is owned in various shares by real own-
> ers, and has nothing to do with debt.[2]

And again:

> The other theory [that is, Fisher's] adopts as
> its intermediary a supposed entity 'The Business.'
> All assets are regarded as 'owing' to The Business
> and The Business is regarded as owing all the 'lia-
> bilities' in which are included the proprietary claims.
> This is a favorit theory in this country, and it has
> this merit that it recognizes that the proprietor or
> proprietors may have many other investments and do not
> in the accounts presented reveal anything more than
> their worth as to The Business. But I cannot see that
> it justifies the inclusion of the proprietorship among
> the liabilities. Surely The Business does not stand
> in the same relation to its proprietors or its capi-
> talists as to its 'other' liabilities. It would seem

---

[1]Irving Fisher, The Nature of Capital and Income
(New York: The Macmillan Company, 1906), p. 92.

[2]Sprague, op. cit., p. 33.

more appropriate to say that it is 'owned by' than 'owes' the proprietors.[1]

Sprague appears to have been repelled not necessarily by Fisher's characterization of the firm as a "fictitious person" (for Sprague himself uses the term "business entity"), but by the economist's insistence that the proprietary equity is a liability of the firm. To Sprague, such an interpretation was not only too abstract a picture of the firm's economic status, but it stretched unnaturally the meaning of "liability." The existence of a liability suggests a maturity date, and the use of such a term for describing proprietorship was contrary to the going-concern assumption that is implicit in Sprague's analysis. Furthermore, at least to Sprague, liabilities are limited to a stipulated sum; proprietorship is not. Writes Sprague, "The right of a creditor is limited to a definit sum which does not shrink when the assets shrink, while that of the proprietor is of an elastic value."[2] But one should be careful not to interpret Sprague's rejection of Fisher's assets = liabilities relation as necessarily a denial also of the separate existence of the firm. To be sure, Sprague's separation of business from personal affairs is an indicium that he opposed a complete merger be-

---

[1] Ibid., p. 49. As a humorous observation in passing, it may be noted that Sprague twice misspells Fisher's first name—and uses two different misspellings. On p. 33, he uses "Irwin" Fisher and on p. 42, he uses "Irvin" Fisher. Although Sprague refers to Fisher elsewhere as "Prof. Fisher" or "Professor Fisher," he does not again use Fisher's first name.

[2] Ibid., p. 47.

tween the two; on the other hand, such a separation *ipso facto* in no way implies the author's desire to establish the firm as the accounting unit.

Fisher's characterization of the whole right-hand side of the balance sheet as "liabilities" is not a necessary part of the conception of the firm as a "fictitious person" for accounting purposes, although a number of early twentieth-century accounting writers so defined "liabilities."[1] Paton, probably the most articulate advocate of the "entity theory," does not choose to classify his "owner's equity" as a liability.[2] By the nature of his counter-argument to Fisher, Sprague would seem to accept the "fictitious person" idea if it came without the assets = liabilities conception of the balance sheet. At bottom, Sprague's disagreement with Fisher is inconclusive in revealing the former's true position as to the "proprietary theory."

Hatfield, it is true, opens his treatise with a chapter stressing the equational relationship, Positive Goods less Negative Goods = Proprietorship.[3] (In his second edition 18 years later, he omits this formulation as well as almost all of the chapter material which had accompanied it

---

[1] George Lisle, *Accounting in Theory and Practice* (Edinburgh: William Green & Sons, 1906), p. 69; and Stephen Gilman, *Principles of Accounting* (Chicago: LaSalle Extension University, 1916), pp. 29, 197.

[2] Paton, *Theory*, chaps. 3 and 4.

[3] Hatfield, *op. cit.*, chap. 1.

in the earlier edition.)[1] This equation proves nothing more, however, than his desire to stress the importance of the proprietary interest. He also states, "Proprietorship represents the net wealth . . . of the proprietor."[2] Yet he lauds an earlier work by Lisle that, like Fisher's, espouses the "personification of the firm" that Hatfield, by implication early in his book, seems to reject.[3]

Like Sprague, Hatfield at times seems to make the proprietor his central figure, and at other times he seems to say that the firm is the focal point. In the face of this apparent vacillation, one must interject: either the enterprise is the accounting unit or it is not. The "proprietary theory" seems to say that <u>it is . . . and it is not. In one sense the assets and liabilities are those of the enterprise, and in another sense they are those of the proprietor. But the proprietor is the central figure; it is his properties for which the accounting is to be made. It only happens that the properties of the proprietor (that are relevant) and those of the enterprise are mutually coextensive.</u> But when Hatfield states, "the Balance Sheet is designed to give an

---

[1] Henry Rand Hatfield, <u>Accounting--Its Principles and Problems</u> (New York: D. Appleton and Company, 1927).

[2] Hatfield, <u>Modern Accounting</u>, p. 14.

[3] Hatfield writes of Lisle's book: "This is perhaps the best single volume treating the entire subject which has appeared in English." <u>Ibid.</u>, p. 33. The "implication" is at p. 22, <u>ibid.</u> For a reference to Lisle's work, see footnote 1, p. 112.

intelligent synopsis of the business,"[1] is it not significant
that he did not say "synopsis of the proprietor's net wealth"?
And might not one argue that to say "proprietorship represents
the proprietor's net wealth" is neither no more nor no less
than to say, as Paton might, that "capital stock and retained
earnings represent the equity of the owners"?

The difference between the "proprietary theory" and
the entity-subject, proprietor-beneficiary view (that is, the
"entity theory" wherein the data are directed at the proprietor) reduces to a matter of tweedledum and tweedledee unless
it can be convincingly demonstrated that one will produce
genuinely different accounting results than will the other.

Newlove and Garner,[2] Vatter,[3] and Kell,[4] unlike other
writers who contrast the "proprietary theory" and "entity
theory," indicate to the reader their conceptions of the impact that the "theories" would have on the other postulates
and principles and concepts in the realm of accounting theory.
A comparison of the specifications of each of these writers
will at the least demonstrate that comparers of these two

---

[1]Ibid., p. 45. And again: "[the Balance Sheet] shows
the financial status of the concern. . . ." At p. 54, ibid.

[2]George Hillis Newlove and S. Paul Garner, Advanced
Accounting, Vol. I: Corporate Capital and Income (2 vols.;
Boston: D. C. Heath and Company, 1951), chap. 1.

[3]William J. Vatter, The Fund Theory of Accounting and
Its Implications for Financial Reports (Chicago: The Univer-
sity of Chicago Press, 1947), chap. 1; and William J. Vatter,
"Corporate Stock Equities--Part I," in Morton Backer (editor),
Handbook of Modern Accounting Theory (New York: Prentice-Hall,
Inc., 1955), pp. 361-83.

[4]Kell, op. cit.

"theories" do not necessarily share similar notions of the
import which each "theory" holds for accounting concepts and
principles. Probably the only safe statement that can be
made is the one put forth by Husband and Thomas:

> . . . accountants may be divided into two groups:
> (1) those who claim that the proprietor owns all
> of the assets but owes certain amounts to creditors,
> and (2) those who hold that both liabilities and
> proprietorship are merely claims against the assets.[1]

But they add:

> The former point of view . . . draws its chief
> support from the sole proprietorship and the part-
> nership where the claims of the creditors are not
> restricted to the assets owned by the business prop-
> er but may be extended to the assets owned by the pro-
> prietors in their private capacities. The latter view-
> point . . . draws its support from the situation ex-
> isting in the corporation where the claims of the lia-
> bilities are usually limited by the value of the
> assets.[2]

Although one is prone to accept this generalization as being
true, such acceptance might imply that the accounting viewpoint should vary according to the legal status of the enterprise. If so, there would be no substantive accounting question. But it must be recalled that while there are large
proprietorships, there are also small corporations. Purely
legal distinctions might be misleading: all corporations are
not large. Economic, not legal, considerations should therefore be paramount. Acceptance of the position implicit in
the latter excerpt from Husband and Thomas must be qualified
to the degree by which the acceptor recognizes that the pos-

---

[1]George R. Husband and Olin E. Thomas, _Principles of
Accounting_ (Boston: Houghton Mifflin Company, 1935), p. 18.

[2]_Ibid._

tulated relationships (that is, between the "proprietary
theory" and proprietorships and partnerships and between the
"entity theory" and corporations) are mere "correlations"
and not inexorable causal ties, that is, presumably each
"theory" can be used for all kinds of business organization.

Based on the writings of Newlove and Garner, Vatter,
and Kell, four broad sets of "implications for accounting
theory" will be critically evaluated:

1. Impact on the periodicity postulate.

2. Impact on the relation between "profit" and "change
    in proprietorship"--that is, the way in which to
    treat proprietary investments and withdrawals.

3. Impact on asset valuation and, conjointly, the
    going-concern postulate.

4. Impact on the timing of the realization of profit
    to the beneficiary.

(1) Periodicity. Newlove and Garner believe that
periodicity is "of no great importance" to "proprietary-theory"
profits but is "of major significance" to "entity-theory" profits.[1] But Sprague devotes a whole chapter to the importance
of "The Period,"[2] and he states that

> the economic accounts should run for a definit time.
> . . . No comparison of one of these summaries [of the
> economic, or nominal accounts] with another can be
> useful unless they cover an equal time. It is there-
> fore the best accounting practice to keep economic ac-
> counts open for the year. . . .[3]

---

[1] Newlove and Garner, op. cit., p. 21, item 10.

[2] Sprague, op. cit., chap. 11.

[3] Ibid., p. 60.

And Hatfield, on page three and without any previous discussion of periodicity, refers to the "fixed fiscal period" as
the time after which a new balance sheet is to be prepared.[1]
Kester writes that "the fiscal period should be, and usually
is, a period of regular length. . . ."[2] Although medievals
apparently adopted periods of irregular length, Paciolo
recommended the annual closing.[3] Thus, if the absence of
periodicity is a holding of the "proprietary theory," the
"proprietary theorists"--going as far back as Paciolo--
evinced no tendency to adopt this aspect of the "theory."

(2) Proprietary Investments and Withdrawals. Neither
Newlove-Garner[4] nor Vatter[5] makes allowance for the exclusion
of investment or disinvestment by the proprietor in describing
the "proprietary theorist's" profit.[6] Profit, according to

---

[1]Hatfield, Accounting, p. 3.

[2]Roy B. Kester, Accounting Theory and Practice (2 vols.;
New York: The Ronald Press Company, 1917-18), I, p. 43.

[3]Frater Lucas Pacioli, "De computis et scripturis."
(Thirty-six chapters from Summa de Arithmetica, Geometria,
Proportione et Proportionalita, Venice, 1494) Translated by
Pietro Crivelli. An Original Translation of the Treatise on
Double-Entry Book-Keeping by Frater Lucas Pacioli (London: The
Institute of Book-Keepers, Ltd., 1924), p. 85.

[4]"Profits are increases in net assets, that is, increases in the net figure of positive and negative properties."
Newlove and Garner, op. cit., p. 21, item 8.

[5]Vatter, Fund Theory, p. 4. Kell, like Newlove-Garner
and Vatter, includes the investment and disinvestment in his
"proprietary-theory" profit. Kell, op. cit., p. 46.

[6]It is possible that Newlove, Garner, and Vatter have
assumed implicitly that an adjustment must be made to eliminate the effects on "profit" of investments and withdrawals.
This writer finds it difficult to believe that they would have
included the net result of such transactions in proprietary--

them, is the net change in proprietorship, whatever the source. But Sprague was careful to eliminate such items from his profit calculations.[1] Kester explicitly excludes such transactions in finding profit, and specifically provides that the proprietor's withdrawal of merchandise is not to be classified as revenue.[2] Hatfield also does not include such items in the determination of profit.[3] Indeed, it is difficult to find any twentieth-century accounting books or articles that <u>do</u> advocate the inclusion of proprietary capital changes in the determination of profit.

    (3) <u>Asset Valuation and Going-Concern</u>. Newlove and Garner state that under the "proprietary theory," profits are properly affected by appraisals of the assets.[4] Balance-sheet values, they say, are usually determined on the assumption of short-term realization, rather than on a going-concern basis.[5] Depreciation, moreover, is related to the preservation of capital.[6] In regard to the latter, no one who has

---

or any--"profit." Nevertheless, they make no express mention of such an adjustment.
    If these writers intended such an implicit assumption, this section, "Proprietary Investments and Withdrawals," may be disregarded.

[1]Sprague, <u>op. cit.</u>, p. 60.

[2]Kester, <u>op. cit.</u>, I, pp. 46, 423-24.

[3]Hatfield, <u>Accounting</u>, chap. 10.

[4]Newlove and Garner, <u>op. cit.</u>, p. 21, item 8, and p. 25.

[5]<u>Ibid.</u>, p. 22, item 14.

[6]<u>Ibid.</u>, p. 22, item 14, and p. 24.

read Hatfield's "What They Say About Depreciation"[1] would
accuse that author of associating a depreciation charge with
the problem of maintaining capital intact. And neither Kester nor Sprague connect depreciation with the maintenance of
capital. To be sure, in what way can a bookkeeping entry for
accumulated depreciation insure against the impairment of
capital?

The Newlove-Garner suggestion that "proprietary theorists" would use current-price valuations in preference to
going-concern valuations is reinforced by Vatter, who sees
the "proprietary theory" as requiring a valuation of the proprietor's interest in the firm by recourse to some kind of
market that would reflect the value of such an ownership interest.[2] Kell, while stating that the "entity theory" would
match costs with revenues, describes the "proprietary theory"
as producing a profit that is "the net increase in owner's
capital during the period. . . ."[3] At best, one might infer
from Kell's distinction that the "proprietary theory" yields
only a haphazardly-determined profit figure without any necessary causal connection between expenses and revenues (as
they are conventionally defined). Too, Kell may intend to
imply--at the other extreme of interpretation--that profit
to the "proprietary theorist" is, like Vatter's notion, the
difference in the market price of his ownership share. Such

---

[1]Henry R. Hatfield, "What They Say About Depreciation,"
The Accounting Review, XI, No. 1 (March, 1936), pp. 18-26.

[2]Vatter, Fund Theory, p. 4.

[3]Kell, op. cit., p. 46.

a valuation technique is hardly in harmony with the going-concern assumption.

And the going-concern assumption was not without its supporters during the early decades of the twentieth century. Hatfield expatiates on the importance of the going-concern assumption to the derivation of proper values;[1] without question, he upheld that assumption. Among those who, prior to 1925, explicitly supported the going-concern approach were Finney,[2] Cole,[3] Kester,[4] Montgomery,[5] Dicksee,[6] Gilman,[7] and Krebs.[8] Other books of that era also reflect a going-concern assumption, although their authors apparently chose to leave the matter of expressing a choice as to assumptions unsaid.[9]

---

[1]Hatfield, Modern Accounting, chaps. 4 and 5.

[2]H. A. Finney, Accounting Principles and Bookkeeping Methods (2 vols.; New York: Henry Holt and Company, 1924), I, p. 275; II, pp. 33-34.

[3]William Morse Cole, Accounts--Their Construction and Interpretation (Boston: Houghton Mifflin Company, 1915), Revised and Enlarged Edition, p. 120 and chap. 13.

[4]Kester, op. cit., II, pp. 83-84.

[5]Robert H. Montgomery, Auditing Theory and Practice (1st ed.; New York: The Ronald Press Company, 1912), p. 119.

[6]Lawrence R. Dicksee, Auditing: A Practical Manual for Auditors (4th ed.; London: Gee & Co., 1900), p. 159.

[7]Gilman, Principles of Accounting, p. 160.

[8]William S. Krebs, Outlines of Accounting (New York: Henry Holt and Company, 1923), pp. 10, 15.

[9]Among these is Paul-Joseph Esquerré, The Applied Theory of Accounts (New York: The Ronald Press Company, 1914). On p. 136, he refers to the going-concern assumption, defines it, and relates it to the assumption for a concern which is about to liquidate. Although he does not explicitly choose one over the other, his later valuations unquestionably derive from the former.

The assumption of continuity of enterprise, or going-concern, is, as already observed, inconsistent with a wholesale[1] application of current-price valuation or liquidation valuation. It was pointed out above that the rise of the conventional "matching concept" could be laid to the concurrent rise in acceptance of the going-concern postulate. Thus, the current-valuation characteristic of the "proprietary theory," made express by Newlove-Garner and Vatter and only implied by Kell, does not appear to have been adopted by the large number of twentieth-century writers, including several "proprietary theorists."

It might be mentioned that the "proprietary theory," particularly in regard to its asset-valuation position, appears to be a throwback to the days when voyages and caravans--ventures as opposed to indefinitely-continuing enterprises--characterized commercial activity. But the growth of depersonalized, institutionalized enterprise, together with the economic efficacy of aggregating large amounts of capital for a single undertaking, ushered in a period in which the assumption of continuity of enterprise was axiomatic. Twentieth-century accounting writers evidenced no inclination to deny

---

[1]Many accountants are of the view that it is not improper to introduce market values that are not accompanied by transactions involving the accounting unit into the accounting records and statements. Probably the most commonplace example is "lower of cost or market" in connection with the valuation of short-term investments and inventories. The textual reference, however, is not to exceptional cases (if indeed these cases are exceptional) such as these, but to a complete application of current market values to the valuation of assets.

this assumption. And given the going-concern assumption, a system composed solely of current-price valuations is untenable. It is ironic, moreover, that among the few early twentieth-century advocates of the accounting recognition of appreciating asset values was the writer who has been a stanch supporter of the "entity theory," W. A. Paton.[1]

(4) <u>Timing of Realization by Beneficiary of Profit</u>. A final implication that warrants comment here is conveyed by a statement by Kell to the effect that since the proprietor is the central accounting figure, profits accrue to him as soon as they accrue to the business.[2] Consequently, a formal transfer, such as a dividend, between the nonentity-business and the proprietor is to be viewed as nothing more than a return of capital. It follows that a stock dividend, or dividend in shares, would serve no accounting purpose. Kell also observes that the separation of capital from income, while not necessary under the "proprietary theory," is of critical importance under the "entity theory."[3] These two statements by Kell would seem to be closely interrelated.

In an article to be analyzed below, Husband makes the point that according to a strict interpretation of the "entity theory," the profit of the entity must be viewed as the entity's equity in itself, not as stockholders' equity in the

---

[1]William Andrew Paton and Russell Alger Stevenson, <u>Principles of Accounting</u> (New York: The Macmillan Company, 1918), chap. 20.

[2]Kell, <u>op. cit.</u>, pp. 45, 83.

[3]<u>Ibid.</u>, p. 46.

entity (or, presumably, in the entity's assets).[1] Husband

notes that "entity theorists" err even in computing a "book

value per share" which includes undistributed profits.[2] As

one investigator has found,[3] accounting practitioners as well

as textbook writers follow a method of accounting for undis-

tributed profits of a corporation that is consistent with

neither the "proprietary theory" nor the "entity theory."

They classify undistributed profits apart from invested cap-

ital, but maintain that the profits are those of the entity

until a formal distribution (that is, a dividend in other

than shares of the distributing corporation) has been effected.[4]

Assuming that Husband's criticism is valid (an assumption

that will be rejected in Chapter V), two reasons would justify

such treatment: (1) the legal necessity of separating profits

---

[1]George R. Husband, "The Corporate-Entity Fiction and
Accounting Theory," The Accounting Review, XIII, No. 3 (September, 1938), especially pp. 243-44.

[2]Ibid.

[3]Clarence George Avery, "An Examination of Certain
Aspects of Variation Between the Entity Theory and Accounting
Practice" (unpublished Master's thesis, Department of Account-
ancy, University of Illinois, 1956); especially chaps. 3 and 4.
By "entity theory," Avery implies the "entity-subject, equities-
beneficiary" view.

[4]". . .Any policy or procedure which tends to obscure
the line of cleavage [between earned surplus and capital stock]
is a departure from standard." (p. 105) "Considerations of
both management and equity call for the reporting of business
income, in the first instance, as enterprise earnings even if
no formal legal action is needed to secure transfer to individual possession." (p. 8) "In measuring the equitable share
of the stockholders, . . . surplus must be combined with the
amount invested." (p. 105) Paton and Littleton, An Introduction to Corporate Accounting Standards.

from invested capital, and (2) the need for a relaxation in

the proscriptions of the "entity theory" in order that an

economic reality as understood by readers of financial state-

ments is not obscured by a strict "entity-theory" balance

sheet and income statement.

The need for distinguishing capital from income for

dividend purposes is well known and does not require ampli-

fication here.[1] The "economic reality" alluded to above is

the commonplace association with stockholders of the reported

income of corporations. "Earnings per share" calculations

are ubiquitous in securities market literature.[2] In the face

of this almost instinctive relation of corporate profits to

residual equity, it would be foolhardy indeed for accountants

to employ a balance-sheet and income-statement structure and

terminology that would tend to defeat one of the major pur-

poses for which these statements are currently used.[3] Account-

ing is, after all, utilitarian. This point was made at the

---

[1]See, for example, George S. Hills, The Law of Accounting and Financial Statements (Boston: Little, Brown and Company,
1957), chap. 4.

[2]"Statistical presentations of periodic net income (or
loss) in terms of earnings per share are commonly used in pro-
spectuses, proxy material, and annual reports to shareholders,
and in the compilation of business earnings statistics for the
press, statistical services, and other publications." "Earnings per Share," Bulletin No. 49, American Institute of Certified Public Accountants (formerly the American Institute of
Accountants), Accounting Research Bulletins, No's. 1-51, prepared by the Committee on Accounting Procedure (New York: American Institute of Certified Public Accountants, 1939-59), pp.
29-36, at p. 29. Footnote omitted.

[3]Computation of book value per share and income per
share are common products of financial analysis.

outset of the study. Accounting nonetheless needs a deductively-derived body of theory in addition to an inductively-derived set of generalizations. But to theorize deductively without considering the practical uses to which theory may be put is, for a practical discipline, of little value. Consequently, this writer cannot agree with Husband who, once having demonstrated that even "entity theorists" do not adhere strictly to (his view of) "entity theory" in accounting for stock dividends, calls for abandonment of the "entity theory" in favor of his "representative [or association]" theory (to be described below).[1] The aforementioned departure from the "entity theory" hardly implies the inadequacy of the entire "theory."

By the same token, were the "proprietary theory" applied to a corporation, a compromise with legal exigencies would demand a relaxation of its proscription that profits realized by the corporation would be instantaneously realized by the stockholders, thus making it unnecessary to separate capital from undistributed profits in the balance sheet. This compromise in itself would not eliminate the "proprietary theory" as a valid interpretation of the orientation postulate. Kell seems to imply that the "proprietary theory's" inability to fit the corporate form is a significant factor toward selection of the "entity theory."[2] With such an implication this writer cannot agree. In the immediately fol-

---

[1] Husband, loc. cit., and George R. Husband, "The Entity Concept in Accounting," The Accounting Review, XXIX, No. 4 (October, 1954), pp. 552-63. See Chapter V for related discussion.

[2] Kell, op. cit., pp. 83-87.

lowing paragraphs, this factor will be viewed as having no normative significance.

It has been the purpose of the foregoing exposition and argument to show that writers who attempt to compare the "proprietary theory" with the "entity theory" have chosen an aboriginal and outdated conception of the former. In no meaningful way in terms of present-day realities, does a "choice" exist between the two. Outside of the fact that a number of twentieth-century accounting writers occasionally remind their readers that "the proprietor owns the business assets and owes the business liabilities," they nevertheless do not accept the implications of the "proprietary theory," as interpreted by such writers as Newlove-Garner (whose observations were in turn culled from the writings of Littleton and Gilman),[1] Vatter, and Kell. Unless one is willing to discard the periodicity and going-concern postulates, therefore, the accounting results produced by what is left of the "proprietary theory" are substantially the same as those of the entity-subject, proprietor-beneficiary approach. Hence, it is this writer's conclusion that the "proprietary theory" as such has little[2] relevance to twentieth-century accounting problems.

Furthermore, these writers as well as others have differed as to their conception of the "entity theory."

---

[1]The distinctions between the "proprietary theory" and "entity theory" reported by Newlove-Garner were "adapted in part from (1933) Littleton 192-203; (1939) Gilman 47-64; (1935) Husband-Thomas 18." Newlove and Garner, op. cit., p. 20, footnote 56.

[2]For possible present-day applications, see pp. 218-19, infra.

Paton, as will be shown, subsumed under his "managerial point
of view" (which is his descriptive title in Accounting Theory
for a version of the "entity theory") the prescript that
profit is to be defined as the return to all capital suppliers.[1]
Kell, agreeing with his former teacher, defines his major premise in terms of the Patonian interpretation, and therefore
arrives at the expected conclusion that the "entity theory"
is the better choice:

> The function of accounting is to provide reliable
> relevant data about the accounting entity. To do
> this an accounting must be made for all property ded-
> icated to the undertaking. The underlying assumptions
> of the entity theory are entirely consistent with the
> basic function of accounting. . . .[2]

Of the writers cited above in connection with their views on
the conception of the "proprietary theory," Vatter[3] concurs
with the Paton formulation of the "entity theory," namely,
that inseparably attached to the "entity theory" is the pro-
viso that profits are defined with respect to all capital
suppliers, not with respect solely to residual equity holders.

But Newlove-Garner disagree. "Profits [under the
"entity theory"] represent an increase in the nonlegal liability of the entity to the proprietor or proprietors due to an
excess of recoveries over outlays."[4] And Gilman writes:

---

[1] Paton, Theory, chap. 3.

[2] Kell, op. cit., p. 195.

[3] Vatter, "Corporate Stock Equities--Part I," op. cit.,
pp. 365-66.

[4] Newlove and Garner, op. cit., p. 21, item 8.

"According to the entity theory, profit is the increase in the amount the entity owes to the proprietor, disregarding capital advances and withdrawals."[1]

Since World War II, these apparently contradictory statements of the "entity theory" have generated a significant amount of literature. Conceptions other than the "proprietary theory" and "entity theory" have also been advanced. Prior to a discussion of these recent developments,[2] however, it is necessary that the very significant contributions of Paton in this regard be presented and evaluated.

Summary and Concluding Arguments

From an examination of the literature on the two "theories," one can discern two distinct aspects of the orientation postulate. First, the subject matter of the accounting process must be defined. Second, the manner in which the accounting data are to be reported must be defined. This writer believes that much of the confusion (and discord) about the orientation postulate has arisen because each of these two aspects has been mistaken for the other.

In order to delineate one from the other, the orientation postulate has been separated into dichotomous parts: a "subject" subpostulate and a "beneficiary" subpostulate. The contrary views on the "entity theory" may thus be expressed by the two possibilities, "entity-subject, proprietor-

---

[1] Gilman, op. cit., p. 48.

[2] See Chapter V.

beneficiary" and "entity-subject, equities-beneficiary." In
diminutive form, they would be "proprietor-beneficiary" and
"equities-beneficiary."

On the basis of the above commentary, which effectively dismisses the "proprietary theory" (that is, proprietor-subject, proprietor-beneficiary) from the debate as to
the proper present-day point of view, this writer submits the
contrasting conceptions of the "entity theory" as two relevant alternatives. Discussion of which alternative is the
more appropriate is presented in Chapter VI. Advocacy of
the equities-beneficiary conception of the "entity theory"
is the Patonian position, which is treated next.

The Patonian "Managerial Point of View"

Because Paton did not engage the "proprietary theorists" on the battleground of asset valuation (and going-
concern), it would appear[1] that he recognized that the "proprietary theory" as it was exposited during the first two
decades of the twentieth century was fully harmonious with
the going-concern and periodicity postulates. As such, it
was only necessary to convince accounting theorists that it
was a small but important step from their majority position

---

[1] Occasionally, however, Paton seems to suggest that
"proprietary theorists" did in fact advocate a different principle of valuation. This inference assumes greater validity
when Paton's criticisms of the "proprietary-theory" accounting results become more severe. For example, he writes, "The
result [of adopting the "proprietary theory"] is a system of
concepts and principles highly inapplicable to the facts of
modern business organization." Paton, Theory, p. 477.

to full-fledged acceptance of the enterprise as the accounting unit. Inasmuch as he was interested chiefly in the corporate form, his argument necessarily had to emphasize the
dominance of that kind of business organization. Thence, he
would argue that the corporation being as important as it
was (and would be), the accounting structure should be revised so as to best effectuate corporate reporting. To complete his restatement, Paton advocates a concept of income
(or profit)[1] which would include the return to all capital
suppliers[2]--not only to residual equity holders. With this
synopsis of the Paton proposal as a preface, a critical sum-
marization of the relevant portions of Paton's treatise
follows.

In the published form of his doctoral dissertation,
Paton explicitly states his purpose:

> . . . to present a restatement of the theory of
> accounting consistent with the conditions and needs
> of the business enterprise par excellence, the
> large corporation, as well as applicable to the
> simpler, more primitive forms of organization.[3]

---

[1]Paton, in his Accounting Theory, uses "net revenue"
instead of net income--a term which he later adopted. Here-
after, as before, "profit," "profits," "income," and "net income" will be used interchangeably, except where noted to the
contrary.

[2]Although Paton's "managerial point of view" embraces
a "return" to long-term capital suppliers only, the term "capital suppliers" will be used in most cases herein without this
qualifying adjective. It seems to this writer, furthermore,
that Paton's "return" might better refer to all capital suppliers, but because the distinction is relatively small and is
inconsequential to most of the subsequent discussion, the a-
forementioned procedure seems justified. The issue is raised
again in Chapter V, in connection with the evaluation of Nammer's "activity concept." See footnote 1, p. 192 , of Chapter V. For Paton's discussion, see Paton, Theory, pp. 260-64.

[3]Ibid., p. iv.

Hence, the full title, <u>Accounting Theory--With Special Ref-</u>
<u>erence to the Corporate Enterprise</u>.

His hypothesis is early stated:

> It is the opinion of the writer that [the] doc-
> trines of proprietorship, as propounded by Sprague,
> Hatfield, and others, are not an entirely adequate
> statement of the theory of accounts under the con-
> ditions of modern business organization.[1]

Here Paton appears to understate somewhat his case. As
is evident in the succeeding pages of his book,[2] he believes
(and one would anticipate that a person of Paton's entity-
philosophy would believe) that proprietorships and partner-
ships--regardless of the stage of capitalistic development--
might also be treated as accounting entities, depending on
the attendant circumstances.

Paton's approach may be divided into two parts, namely,
A. To ascertain the accountant's point of view as to subject
matter; and B. To develop a theory of financial reporting
that is consistent with the result of A. and that meets the
requirements of modern enterprise.

A. <u>The Accounting Unit</u>. The Patonian argument is
that the business enterprise is the relevant accounting unit.[3]
It is significant to the thesis of the present study that
Paton, although he uses inconsistent terminology in the early

---

[1] Ibid., p. iii.

[2] Especially at pp. 16-18, ibid.

[3] Paton's argument, which need not be developed here,
is presented in chap. 1, ibid. Also see pp. 472-78, ibid.

pages of his treatise,[1] recognizes that (1) the proprietary-
entity question is one of assumption and not of concept,[2] and
(2) the formulation of an accounting postulate or assumption
must be in harmony with the overlay of principle. As to the
latter, Paton writes (in spite of the unfortunate choice of
terms, his meaning is clear):

> Accounting classifications and procedures are
> significant only as they are related to the con-
> ditions of the specific business organization.
> Here we have the underlying conception of the ac-
> countant, a conception which conditions the entire
> accounting structure.[3]

And although an occasional statement[4] seems to belie this interpretation, it is Paton's view that economic necessity, not
legal recognition, is the test of sufficiency for accounting
acceptance of the business enterprise as its unit. In almost
so many words, he asserts that the business enterprise (= accounting unit) is a reality, not a fiction.[5] In sum, his position as to the first subpostulate is squarely behind the

---

[1]For example, he calls the proprietary point of view
a "concept" and "doctrine." Ibid., p. iii.

[2]This view is evident in chaps. 3 and 20, ibid.

[3]Ibid., p. 17.

[4]See, for example, p. 19, ibid.

[5]"The business enterprise is a reality, an important
economic institution, and is certainly of the utmost significance in the field of accounting." Ibid., p. iv. But many
pages later: "On the other hand, there is a danger that this
assumption may be carried too far. The fact of the independent existence of the business entity must not be overstressed.
No institution, however real, has any absolute existence."
Ibid., p. 476. If one accepts this important qualification,
the strict entity view that Husband says is representative of
the conceptions of "entity theorists" is less defensible. See
above, footnote 1, p. 125, and below, Chapter V.

entity view. He would make exceptions depending on the circumstances, but since his discussion deals mostly with the corporation, particularly the large corporation, he assumes tacitly through most of the exposition that such mitigating circumstances are not present.

B. _The Overlay of Accounting Theory_. Given the business enterprise as the accountant's center of attention for data-accumulation purposes, ". . . shall the proprietary or the managerial point of view be adopted in stating the theory of accounts?"[1]

Paton begins his argument by stating:

> If proprietorship is the fundamental and pivotal concept for the accountant in dealing with modern business transactions, the interpretation of expense and revenue (or 'profit and loss') items and accounts as direct accessories of proprietorship naturally follows. The expiration of labor and materials purchased by the enterprise and consumed in putting out its product becomes a charge of the same general significance as the net return on all capital invested by other interests than the proprietary. It is at this point, the writer believes, that the doctrines of proprietorship have led to serious error. The commonly accepted conceptions of the operating accounts advanced by the proponents of proprietary accounting have tended to shut the door to all discriminating analysis of the income sheet. As a result the average income sheet is a hodge-podge of illogical, non-illuminating classifications. The importance of revision of accounting theory at this point is acute. The income sheet of the large corporation, certainly, is not an adjunct of any single interest or equity in the balance sheet, to be defined in terms of that interest; and any attempt to view it so results in distortion of so serious a character as largely to destroy the utility of the statement.[2]

---

[1] Paton, _Theory_, p. 52.

[2] _Ibid._, pp. 52-53; footnote omitted.

His "managerial point of view" also calls for the characterization of the entire right-hand side of the balance sheet as
"equities." Unlike a number of earlier writers who sought to
merge the liability and proprietorship classifications, Paton
does not describe the combined grouping as "liabilities."[1]
His argument for a homogenized right-hand side of the balance
sheet, which, to Paton was married to his proposal that profit
be determined with respect to all capital suppliers, may be
summed up as follows:

> In economics the property-holder, investor, is
> commonly thought of as furnishing two principal con-
> ditions or functions in production: (1) risk and re-
> sponsibility-taking, and (2) 'waiting power'--pure
> capital service. . . . All economic characteristics
> found in connection with any equity attach in some
> degree to every other equity. . . .
>   We are dealing here not with fundamental distinc-
> tions but merely with differences in degree. The
> individual or interest that assumes the larger ele-
> ments of risk in a business enterprise, and takes the
> major share of responsibility and control, approxi-
> mates the economist's 'entrepreneur' and the account-
> ant's 'proprietor'; the individual or interest that
> furnishes capital but takes comparatively little risk,
> and has but slight or indirect control of ordinary
> operations, approaches the economist's 'capitalist
> proper' and the accountant's 'creditor.' But it can-
> not be stated too emphatically that every equity,
> proprietary or otherwise, furnishes capital (money,
> commodities, or services);[2] every equity involves
> risk of loss; virtually all equities have some priv-
> ileges and responsibilities with respect to manage-
> ment; and all long-term equities have rights in in-
> come and capital.
>   To sum up: property ownership connotes such at-
> tributes as control, title, risk-taking, and capital
> furnishing. No one of these elements attaches ex-

---

[1] For comment, see pp. 137-139.

[2] [Footnote in original:] "With, perhaps, the single
exception of what we may call the state's equity." Paton,
Theory, p. 61, footnote 10.

clusively to what the accountant labels 'proprietorship' as opposed to liabilities. Consequently we can
conclude that ownership or equities constitutes a
class rationally comprehending both of these divisions.[1]

The changing character of corporate enterprise (and
of corporate securities), according to Paton, permits a less
and less clear division between liabilities and owners' equity.[2] Berle and Means, a decade later, added weight to this
thesis:

> Though the law still maintains the conception
> of a sharp dividing line recognizing the bondholder
> as a lender of capital and the stockholder as a
> quasi-partner in the enterprise, economically the
> positions of the two have drawn together. Conse-
> quently, security holders may be regarded as a
> hierarchy of individuals all of whom have supplied
> capital to the enterprise, and all of whom expect
> a return from it.[3]

After taking the position that A = E is better than
either A - L = P or A = L + P, Paton argues that his "managerial point of view" is probably less applicable to sole
proprietorships and partnerships than it is to "business
enterprise par excellence," the large corporation.[4] (This
point involves both Parts A. and B., as divided here, of his
exposition.) He does not deny that the economic entity should
be singled out and accounted for as a unit, but the lack of
legal-entity status for proprietorships and partnerships seems

---

[1]Ibid., pp. 60-61; emphasis in original; one footnote
omitted.

[2]For Paton's discussion, see pp. 75-84, ibid.

[3]Berle and Means, op. cit., p. 279.

[4]See pp. 61-68 and 84, Paton's Theory.

to dissuade him from advocating <u>without reservation</u> the "managerial point of view" for these organizations. Instead, he would countenance a "proprietary" (this writer's proprietor-beneficiary) accounting--glorifying the proprietorship category, although he nonetheless prefers the application of the "managerial point of view" even to these kinds of situations wherever feasible.[1]

That Paton does not insist rigidly on a universal application of his "managerial point of view" is estimable. His line of demarcation, however, is subject to question. Paton appears to be skeptical of the applicability of the "managerial point of view" to unincorporated enterprises: situations in which the enterprise is not a <u>legal</u> entity and, therefore, in which the assets are <u>legally</u> owned (and liabilities <u>legally</u> owed) by the owners. Furthermore, he suggests, the creditors of a failing <u>unincorporated</u> enterprise could look <u>legally</u> to the owners, not solely to the firm, for satisfaction. Is such a situation consistent, he seems to ask, with interpreting that enterprise (that is, unincorporated enterprise in general) as an accounting entity? In response, it would seem that the circumstances in which creditors would look not to the firm, but to the owners, for payment of their debts would also be circumstances in which the going-concern assumption is not valid. A more critical test, and one which

---

[1]Paton's criteria for "feasible" seem to vary from wholly legal factors to the other pole of wholly economic factors. Consult chap. 1 and pp. 476-77, <u>ibid</u>.

embodies the going-concern assumption, would turn on the
economic character of the enterprise--regardless of its legal
status.[1] Paton might better have said: For a firm in which
sufficient dispersal of ownership and managerial constituents
requires that one group be accountable to the other, prima
facie evidence exists for recognition of the firm as a self-
contained unit for data-accumulation as well as reporting
purposes (suggesting, in turn, that "profit" is the return
to all capital suppliers). Where, on the other hand, the
owner is also the manager, the personal attachment between
owner and business may be so great as to render an entity
conception of the firm for reporting purposes an unjusti-
fiable interpretation of the facts.[2]

Insistence on a juxtaposition of assets with a homogenized interest therein, that is, equities, endeavors to
defeat the fractionalization of the right-hand side of the
balance sheet into "liabilities" and "proprietorship." It
is important to note that in addition to exemplifying a
stricter entity approach (in the sense of equities-beneficiary),
the "assets = equities" conception of the firm's status also
represents a more rigorous and complete application of the

---

[1]This is not to disdain legal considerations when conceiving the accounting unit. As indicated in Chapter III (pp.
81-83), above, accounting is concerned with economic phenomena.
To the extent that legal phenomena influence the character of
economic phenomena, the former are unquestionably relevant to
accounting questions.

[2]This is not to say, however, that such a factual situation militates against the use of the business enterprise as
the accounting unit (that is, for data-accumulation purposes).

going-concern postulate. The A = L + P conception in effect
clothes only the net assets (that is, assets less liabilities)
with a full-fledged going-concern mantle.[1] A quantum (as opposed to a res) of assets equal to the amount of liabilities
is implicitly presumed to be devoted not to the enterprise,
but to (the satisfaction of) its creditors. Only the residual
quantum of assets is identified with the continuity of the
enterprise--the enduring owner's equity. That this is a valid interpretation may be suggested by an examination of the
various balance-sheet equations. The A = L + P formulation
(or especially the alternative of A - L = P, which seems to
have been the preferable form of expression for a number of

---

[1]It has been suggested that such a holding would require that the "non-going-concern" portion of the assets
(that is, that amount which equals the amount of the liabilities) must be revalued at current prices. This operation
is impossible to accomplish except in rare situations, where,
for example, the current price of the total of all assets is
the same per cent above or below the recorded value as is
that for every asset item. In the great majority of situations, since specific asset items cannot be related to specific right-hand items, one cannot know which asset values
to adjust to current prices.
     The suggestion is indeed appealing, but not persua-
sive. (If the suggestion were valid, it would cast doubt on
the feasibility of any approach that embraced the A = L + P
conception.) It would seem that the question of "going concern" relates to the entire accounting unit; implications of
the going-concern assumption for principles and concepts, it
would follow, should be for the whole unit. Other accounting expressions, reflecting either postulates or principles
and concepts, should be in harmony with the going-concern
assumption--if the latter is accepted as valid. The crux of
this writer's comment, in the text, is that the A = L + P
expression does not appear to be in harmony with the going-
concern assumption.

early twentieth-century writers)[1] seems to say that "assets
of $xxx are available to meet creditors' claims, after which
the balance of the assets is left for the owners (or, alternatively, is left for the firm)." "Assets = equities," on
the other hand, suggests that the assets do not have a multitude of "loyalties," but exist only for the good of the
entirety, or the enterprise. All assets are treated as though
they were going-concern assets. All assets are identified
with the firm. Hence, both the entity and going-concern postu-
tulates receive greater emphasis in the revised conception
of enterprise status.

Paton would then say that it follows from this iden-
tification of all assets with the totality of the enterprise
that accounting should provide a measure of the effectiveness

---

[1]See, for example, Hatfield, Modern Accounting, chap.
1. Kester even arranged his balance-sheet illustrations according to the format of A - L = P. Kester, op. cit., I, pp.
30, 34, 35, 240; he calls this report-form statement, "financial statement." Later, when he introduces the account form
of the balance sheet (which he titles "balance sheet"), he
utilizes the arrangement of A = L + P. Ibid., p. 241.
Indeed, Canning writes in as late as 1929: "All economists are familiar with the expression, 'assets less liabilities equals proprietorship.' This, stated in one form or
another, is what accountants call the fundamental equation of
accounts." John B. Canning, The Economics of Accountancy: A
Critical Analysis of Accounting Theory (New York: The Ronald
Press Company, 1929), p. 11. Therein, Canning criticizes
Paton's reformulation: "Those writers who urge consideration
of liabilities as negative assets express a view more fruitfully suggestive than do those who habitually associate liabilities and net proprietorship [that is, proprietorship;
Canning allows "gross proprietorship" to equal total assets]
in their discussion." Ibid., pp. 50-51; footnote omitted;
emphasis in original.

with which <u>all</u> of the assets have been utilized--or, in other
words, a measure of the effectiveness with which <u>all</u> of the
interests have been served. The profit figure would then be
redefined in terms of the various claimants in accord with
(1) the contractual limitations of the claims, and (2) the
paramountcy of the claims <u>inter sese</u>. Each claimant's share
would, in effect, be credited to his equity classification
until the entire equity side, enhanced by a dollar amount
equal to the dollar-amount enhancement in assets during the
period (other than by investment or disinvestment by any of
the claimants), would be necessarily equal in dollar amount
to the dollar amount of assets.

At the time of its unveiling, the Patonian conception
of net income was, to say the least, unique. This writer
has been unable to find a similar interpretation in the pre-
Paton accounting literature.[1] By unanimous consent, net in-

[1]As a joint author with R. A. Stevenson, Paton first
revealed his "managerial point of view" (although this term
was first used in his <u>Theory</u>) in an elementary text in 1917.
William A. Paton and Russell A. Stevenson, <u>Principles of Ac-
counting</u> (Ann Arbor, Mich.: George Wahr, 1917). This treatise was expanded for republication in the following year.
Paton and Stevenson, <u>Principles of Accounting</u>, 1918, <u>loc.
cit</u>. In the latter, the authors' statement of policy was
forthrightly put:
"In the first place it has seemed to the authors
that the importance of the <u>proprietary</u> interest, so-
called, is unduly stressed in most textbooks. Indeed,
the usual treatment of the subject is so dominated by
the doctrines of proprietorship that it might well be
described as 'proprietary accounting.' Although this
theory of accounts is not an unreasonable view for the
accountant who is dealing with very simple situations,
as applied to the complex conditions of modern business
organization it becomes practically untenable." (p. vii)

come had been viewed unquestioningly as relating to only the
proprietary equity--in those writings where the author made
known his preference. Some writers suggested by their illustrations that almost every balance that was struck was a kind
of profit, serving effectively to blur the reader's conception of the meaning of that term. Esquerré, for example,
gives this form (outlined here) of the income statement:[1]

Stanley E. Howard, in a review of the 1918 text, dis-
dains the authors' innovation. Howard reacted unfavorably to
the authors' contention that current liabilities could be
viewed as equities "only in a limited sense." See, ibid., p.
315. "Liabilities of this kind," Paton and Stevenson write,
"usually do not assume significance in amount, and hence do
not represent an important element in the ownership of the
enterprise." Ibid., p. 318. As to the classification of all
liabilities, Howard argues, however: "This concept of liabilities as equities, if not exactly fantastic, is, then, of du-
bious usefulness." Stanley E. Howard, Review of Principles
of Accounting, by William Andrew Paton and Russell Alger Stevenson, The American Economic Review, IX, No. 3 (September,
1919), 563-66, at p. 565.
Howard was not the only contemporary dissenter. J.
T. Madden, in a review of Paton's 1924 elementary text, writes,
after first citing the Sprague approach, "We question whether
this term [i.e., equities], which has come to have a very definite connotation in law, should be used in accounting in the
way Professor Paton has done." J. T. Madden, Review of Accounting, by W. A. Paton, Publications of the American Association of University Instructors in Accounting, IX, No. 2
(December, 1925), pp. 158-59.

[1]Esquerré, op. cit., pp. 433-37. Esquerré's illustration is that of the "Black Diamond Manufacturing Company,"
which this writer has been unable to establish as an actual
firm. It was the practice of text writers during the first
two decades of the twentieth century, however, to cite the
financial statements of actual concerns rather than offer a
model form.

Statement of Income and Profit and Loss

Income from Sales
Less: Cost of Goods Sold
Gross Profit on Sales
Less: Selling Expense
Selling Profit
Less: Administrative and General Expenses
Profit from Operations
Add: Additions to Income
Total
Less: Deductions from Income
Gross [sic!] Profit and Income from Operating
   and Other Sources
Less: Extraordinary Losses of the Period
Net Profit for the Year
Less: Reserved [that is, net increases in surplus
   reserves]
Profit and Loss Surplus at [end of year]
Add: Surplus at [beginning of year]
Surplus at [end of year]

Paton and Stevenson use four concepts of "net revenue"
(that is, net income): net revenue from operation, total net
revenue, net revenue to private equities, and proprietary net
revenue.[1] It is not reprehensible *per se* that net income is
used in several different contexts; it is bad, however, when
(1) the phraseology is vague and inconsistent, and (2) the
different concepts are not carefully and clearly distinguished
from each other in the accompanying textual discussion.[2]

---

[1]Paton and Stevenson, *Principles of Accounting*, 1918,
p. 553.

[2]Among the few pre-Paton writers who investigated in
some depth the nature of the profit calculation were Hatfield,
Modern Accounting, chaps. 11, 12, and 15; and Cole, *op. cit.*,
pp. 342-46. Cole, developing further an earlier inquiry by
Lisle (*op. cit.*, pp. 49-50), discusses how accountants might
allocate the proprietor's profit among proprietary wages, interest, and return for risk. In this respect, Cole partially
anticipates the Patonian discussion of the income-statement
segregation of *explicit* salary, interest, and return for
risk--where the former two are contractually provided for,
particularly as regards a corporation.

Paton and Stevenson, as might be expected, did probe rather deeply--for an introductory text--into the meanings and import of the various concepts of "net revenue."

Contemporary Criticism in Accounting Literature of the Patonian Equities-Beneficiary View

Surprisingly, or perhaps it could have been expected, the new formulation elicited almost no written comment within the first five years of its publication. Two reasons explain this lacuna in the unfolding of the literature of the orientation postulate. First, The Accounting Review had not yet been launched,[1] and the only other major American accounting periodical, The Journal of Accountancy, generally seems to have avoided manuscripts on what might have been regarded as esoteric sojourns into theory. Furthermore, the progenitor of the American Accounting Association, the American Association of University Instructors in Accounting, did not commence publishing book reviews until 1925. Second, it is likely that few accountants understood and appreciated the Patonian restatement. Very little theoretical analysis of the rigorous deductive type had appeared prior to 1922. Paton's treatise seems to have occupied what was previously a vacuum more so than it did to displace the findings of other deeply theoretical researches.

The single review of Accounting Theory that this writer has unearthed was written by Willard H. Lawton, a

---

[1] The first number appeared in March, 1926.

Pennsylvania C.P.A. who contributed numerous book reviews to the Journal from 1915 to 1936. Relative to the word "equities," Lawton comments:

> As a manner of nomenclature it would be welcomed by the profession no doubt, though it is not at all likely that it will supersede the time-honored present title [that is, "liabilities"] in the business world. As a scientific term it is accurate and has its proper place in a scientific theory.[1]

It is significant that Lawton also observes the following:

> The curious thing is . . . that if we admit the author's premise--that the business itself is an entity or personality--there is apparently no logical reason why the old title, 'liabilities,' should not be retained. If it is assumed that the business is entirely distinct and separable from the proprietor, then it would be a perfectly logical deduction that the net worth is the amount owed by the business to the proprietor. But this is of minor importance.[2]

In what appears to be the only published comment by Hatfield of Paton's restatement,[3] he writes:

---

[1] W. H. Lawton, Review of Accounting Theory--With Special Reference to the Corporate Enterprise, by William Andrew Paton, The Journal of Accountancy, XXXV, No. 4 (April, 1923), pp. 313-14, at p. 314.

[2] Lawton implies the full-fledged personification of the enterprise that Paton wished to avoid (see footnote 5, p. 132). Ibid.

[3] In conversation with this writer, Paton indicated that in neither published form nor personal correspondence did he or Hatfield analyze the other's orientation-postulate position with a view toward either sharpening the lines of demarcation or reconciling their disparate approaches. The below-quoted excerpt from a book review by Hatfield is the only evidence that this writer has been able to find of either writer's commenting directly on the thesis of the other. Personal Interviews with William A. Paton, March, 1961.

Professor Paton places some emphasis on his chosen
formula for bookkeeping, that is, assets = equities,
as against that made familiar by Sprague, assets =
liabilities + proprietorship. The change is not one
to which any particular objection can be made. But
it is possible that he, with pardonable prejudice,
overestimates the significance of this innovation,
for he states: 'It must be borne in mind that two
quite distinct elements are included under the head
of equities, proprietorship and liabilities,' (page
73). To some it would seem that there is little
significant difference between saying that the right-
hand side of the balance-sheet contains two distinct
categories, liabilities and proprietorship, and saying that it contains only equities, but these are divided into 'two quite distinct elements.'[1]

The excerpt that Hatfield quotes (coming, as it does, from a
book that Paton wrote two years after the publication of his
Theory) appears also to be a partial retreat from Paton's
earlier position that holds, in effect, that liabilities and
proprietorship are probably indistinguishable for the large
corporation, and even if they are distinguishable, they should
not be distinguished.

Hatfield concludes his comments as follows:

There is only one point in the book which the
present reviewer cares to criticize. This is the
adoption of the term 'net income' as the balance
of earnings from which both interest and dividends
are to be subtracted. Net income, as used by the
interstate commerce commission, is a pretty well
crystallized term. It seems unnecessarily confus-
ing to use it now with an entirely different content. Professor Paton argues most soundly that
the balance which he calls 'net income' is of
great significance and its amount should be brought
clearly to the attention of those reading an income
statement. Perhaps 'gross income,' the term used
by the commission, is not entirely satisfactory to
Professor Paton. But one who had the originality
to devise the term 'equities,' would surely have
been able to think up some new term rather than

[1]Henry Rand Hatfield, Review of Accounting, by W. A.
Paton, The Journal of Accountancy, XL, No. 5 (November, 1925),
p. 389.

146

to use an old term with a new meaning.[1]
That Hatfield would be so amenable to the Patonian restatement reinforces this writer's view that the so-called "proprietary theorists" of the early twentieth century were
never very far from the principles of income determination
which are in harmony with the entity-subject, proprietor-
beneficiary postulate. Save for differences in handling
certain returns to capital suppliers, they were not very
far from the Paton formulation.

The validity of Hatfield's concluding criticism of
Paton's concept of net income will be evaluated in Chapter
VI.

---

[1]Ibid., p. 390. These comments by Hatfield will, in
the context of this study, prove to be prophetic.

CHAPTER V

A CRITICAL SURVEY OF SELECTED RECENT

COMMENTARY ON THE ORIENTATION

POSTULATE

In the last thirty-five years, and particularly
since World War II, a number of new orientation-postulate
formulations as well as criticisms of previously-expounded
formulations have been articulated in varying degrees of
lucidity. In the words of Sprouse, who has been one of the
very few to attempt to reconcile the disparate views:

> Criticisms of existing theories have tended to
> be vague and general. Indictments such as that the
> proprietary theory is 'seriously defective' as a
> framework for corporation accounting [footnote cit-
> ing Paton], that 'neither the proprietary theory
> nor the entity theory is a wholly satisfying frame
> of reference for accounting' because each relies
> upon a 'personality' [footnote citing Vatter], and
> that the 'two traditional frames of reference that
> are found in accounting theory' are inadequate
> [footnote citing Suojanen], have not been supported
> by demonstrations of the undesirable results of ac-
> counting analyses based on the corporate concepts
> to which objections are made.
> Furthermore, irreconcilable conflicts of inter-
> pretation, inadequately explained, appear in the
> literature.[1]

---

[1] Robert T. Sprouse, "The Significance of the Concept
of the Corporation in Accounting Analyses," The Accounting
Review, XXXII, No. 3 (July, 1957), p. 369. See also the
three recent articles by David H. Li: "The Nature of Corporate Residual Equity under the Entity Concept," The Accounting
Review, XXXV, No. 2 (April, 1960), pp. 258-63; "The Nature
and Treatment of Dividends under the Entity Concept," The

It is the purpose of this chapter to present and evaluate some of the more unique innovations and trenchant criticisms. No attempt will be made to be comprehensive in either presentation or evaluation, for volumes could be (and have been) written on many of the conceptions. The foregoing presentations and commentaries purport only to be indicative of the crosscurrents of thinking on the matter of "a point of view for accounting."

The first section of the chapter will deal somewhat expansively with the interpretation of the income-tax charge under the equities-beneficiary approach--a subject on which a goodly amount has been written. The remainder of the chapter will be divided according to the contributions chosen, on an author-by-author basis. This manner of organization has been deemed most effective for expositing the varietal viewpoints.

The Location of Income Taxes in the Income Statement

In examining the literature on the subject of accounting for income taxes, one is impressed by the singular lack of a meeting of the minds on many aspects of the problem. If writers would first make explicit their concept of net income

---

Accounting Review, XXXV, No. 4 (October, 1960), pp. 674-79; and "Income Taxes and Income Tax Allocation under the Entity Concept," The Accounting Review, XXXVI, No. 2 (April, 1961), pp. 265-68.

Full footnote references have been omitted from the Sprouse excerpt; Paton's views are presented in Chapter IV; the views of Vatter and Waino W. Suojanen are exposited in this chapter.

(deriving, in part, from their notion of the orientation postulate)--as a major premise--the merit of competing arguments would be more apparent. Instead, proprietor-beneficiary exponents do not reveal (explicitly) their allegiance while developing their arguments--which lead to the conclusion, to be expected, that income taxes are a pre-net income item. Then, it seems, an equities-beneficiary adherent, again without showing his colors, replies that income taxes are properly a distribution of net income. Often the dispute then enters upon the battleground of "all-inclusive income statements versus current-operating-performance income statements."[1] As will be noted below, disagreements over the desirability of intra-period and inter-period tax allocation might also be traceable to different concepts of net income, originating in turn from different views of the orientation postulate.

Truly, a multi-volume work could be assembled on the nature and income-statement presentation of income taxes. Much has already been written, including several doctoral dissertations, on the problem of inter-period tax allocation alone. The following paragraphs attempt to survey rather

---

[1]It would seem that either of these two conceptions could be adopted for income statements irrespective of whether the entity-subject, proprietor-beneficiary or entity-subject, equities-beneficiary view is selected as the orientation postulate. For discussion of the characteristics and relative merits of the all-inclusive and current-operating-performance conceptions, see American Institute of Certified Public Accountants (formerly the American Institute of Accountants), "Income and Earned Surplus," Bulletin No. 32 (December, 1947) Accounting Research Bulletins, 1-51, prepared by the Committee on Accounting Procedure (New York: American Institute of Certified Public Accountants, 1939-59), pp. 259-66.

discursively some of the basic issues as they relate to the equities-beneficiary subpostulate and the consequent concept of net income.

It is not necessary to examine at length the reaction of advocates of the proprietor-beneficiary school to the Patonian (pre-1943)[1] treatment of income taxes. They would certainly classify income taxes as a deduction in arriving at the return to owners--which they would naturally label as net income. Except where noted to the contrary, therefore, the following views on income-tax location presuppose the acceptance of the equities-beneficiary approach.

Vatter, in examining the concept of net income which would seem to emerge logically from the equities-beneficiary view, observes, "Taxes on net income . . . would seem to fall in the category of distributions of income rather than determinants of 'profit.'"[2] He offers no argumentation, however, to support this position.

In his Accounting Theory,[3] Paton, not without some misgivings, classifies income taxes as a distribution of "net revenue" (that is, net income). He offers the following illustration of the "Net Revenue Division":[4]

---

[1]The significance of the year 1943 is indicated on pp. 151-152.

[2]As in Chapter IV, "profit" in this chapter will be used interchangeably with the following terms: "profits," "income," and "net income."

[3]William Andrew Paton, Accounting Theory--With Special Reference to the Corporate Enterprise (New York: The Ronald Press Company, 1922).

[4]Ibid., pp. 269-70; see also pp. 179-81, ibid.

NET REVENUE DIVISION, INCOME SHEET OF X CO., DEC. 31, 19--

OPERATING NET REVENUE	$......	
Interest Earned	....	$......
Fire Loss		....
NET REVENUE TO ALL EQUITIES, Before Deducting Taxes		$......
Interest on Mortgage Bonds	$	
Interest on Debentures	....	
Interest on Notes	....	......
		$......
Federal Income and Profits Taxes		....
		$......
Preferred Dividends		....
NET BALANCE FOR COMMON STOCK		$ ....
Common Dividends		....
Undivided Profits		$ ....
Surplus Balance, Jan. 1, 19--		.....
		$ .....
Reserve for Contingencies		....
TOTAL UNAPPROPRIATED SURPLUS, Dec. 31, 19--		$ .....

Two years later, Paton was less equivocal: "The allowance for
Federal income taxes . . . is deducted from net income."[1]

Over the years, Paton has retained essentially the
same format--after allowance is made for changes in terminology. In 1943, however, he decided that the governmental
levy had become too large to permit the computation of any
meaningful net income figure prior to the subtraction of income taxes. In his words:

> The terms 'net income' and 'net profit,' by long
> usage, imply the amount of earnings available for
> owners or investors, and are not at all appropriate
> to describe figures which may be eight or ten times
> the size of actual net corporate income or profits.
> As long as income and profits taxes were of rela-
> tively small amount the reporting of such taxes as
> a prior participation in the net income produced by
> the corporation was not particularly objectionable;
> under present conditions such reporting may be def-
> initely misleading. To report 'net profit before
> income and profits taxes' of $50,000,000, for ex-

---

[1]W. A. Paton, Accounting (New York: The Macmillan
Company, 1924), p. 465.

ample, when such taxes amount to say $40,000,000,
and actual net corporate income is only $10,000,000,
borders on the fantastic.[1]

And again:

There simply are no _profits_ in any appropriate
sense--at least as far as corporate reporting to
stockholders is concerned--until the processes by
which the total government recovery is determined
have been fully applied.[2]

It had been only two years earlier that Paton's model income
statement exhibited income taxes as a deduction _from_ net income (to all equities).[3] In the same treatise, he termed
"questionable" the grouping of income taxes with other taxes[4]
--a practice which he came to condone two years later. Hence,
although Paton endeavored in 1943 to show that the revision
was induced solely by a new set of facts, it nevertheless reflects at least a partial change in concept.

In 1928, Greer's _How to Understand Accounting_,[5] a
thoughtful short-course aimed at business executives, evidenced

---

[1]William A. Paton, "Adaptation of the Income Statement
to Present Conditions," _The Journal of Accountancy_, LXXV, No. 1
(January, 1943), p. 13.

[2]_Ibid_.

[3]W. A. Paton, _Advanced Accounting_ (New York: The Macmillan Company, 1941), p. 25.

[4]_Ibid_., p. 39. In his most recent book, Paton groups
together _all_ taxes, other than those that relate to the manufacturing process, in a subdivision of "Revenue Deductions"
entitled "Taxes." It is this writer's opinion that Paton's
purpose for this method of presentation is to emphasize the
magnitude of the total tax burden on the firm. William A.
Paton and Robert L. Dixon, _Essentials of Accounting_ (New York:
The Macmillan Company, 1958), pp. 385-86.

[5]Howard C. Greer, _How to Understand Accounting_ (New
York: The Ronald Press Company, 1928).

agreement with the pre-1943 Paton. The following excerpts
effectively convey Greer's conception of the income-tax
deduction:

> Income tax is a more difficult item to handle
> adequately, but there seems no strong argument for
> treating it as an operating expense, and no valid
> objection to considering it a distribution of in-
> come. If this view be adopted it is, of course,
> necessary to assume that the government is, in a
> sense, a contributor of capital to the enterprise,
> and that the tax represents its return on this cap-
> ital. This is a somewhat philosophical conception,
> but entirely practical as a working hypothesis.[1]
> The taxes referred to in the above phrase may
> have their position explained easily enough so long
> as they are income taxes, or taxes based primarily
> on income.[2]

Greer also includes a chart which demonstrates his conception
of the interrelation between the balance sheet and income
statement. It is reproduced here as Figure 1, for it is, in
this writer's opinion, an excellent graphic portrayal of a
consanguinity that eludes many students of accounting theory.

Although Paton had by then reclassified income taxes
as a deduction prior to net income, Greer in 1945 reaffirmed
his 1928 position. Interestingly, the same factor which was
a significant contributor--that is, the huge tax burden of
the war years--toward Paton's reclassification strengthened
Greer's conviction that income taxes are a distribution of
net income. Writes Greer in 1945:

> The concept of an 85-per-cent excess profits tax
> as a 'cost of doing business' is somewhat strained.
> The average corporation has no other cost of so large
> and uncertain amount. There is no possibility of in-
> cluding such an item in calculations of product costs,

---

[1]Ibid., pp. 182-83.   [2]Ibid., p. 185.

154

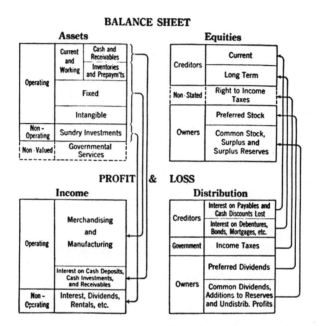

Source: Figure 25, p. 180, in Howard C. Greer, How to Understand Accounting (New York: The Ronald Press Company, 1928).

Fig. 1.--Relation between the balance sheet and income statement, as viewed by Greer.

or in measuring the profitableness of individual
product prices. The performance of such a factor
in a series of cost calculations would be so erratic
and unpredictable that it could not be treated like
any ordinary cost, either in calculations or in
policy-making.

It might be argued that a tax based on gross income should be regarded as a fee for the privilege
of doing business and treated accordingly. Even a
tax on net income, if of very minor amount, might
be similarly handled. Income and profits taxes on
the scales now current are far too large for inclusion among costs of operation without distorting
them beyond significance or usefulness.[1]

Greer concludes that the government is better envisaged as an

equity-holder than as a supplier of goods or services:

The concept of the government as owner of a
share in the corporate enterprises created under
its authority can be harmonized with other accounting concepts without too great difficulty. It is
true that the 'equity' of the government does not
appear with any stated 'value' on the liability
side [sic] of the balance sheet. This, however,
may be said merely to reflect the fact that 'equity'
of the government is not in the property, but in
the earnings, of the corporation.[2]

Greer's last comment is open to serious question. The notion

of an "equity-holder" who does not contribute funds is an

ethereal one indeed.[3] Creditors (other than the government

in respect of taxes) and stockholders seek an equity in prof-

its--as does the government--but they also furnish funds. To

the extent that it is desirable that "equities" consist of a

---

[1]Howard C. Greer, "Treatment of Income Taxes in Corporation Income Statements," The Accounting Review, XX, No. 1
(January, 1945), pp. 97-98.

[2]Ibid., p. 97.

[3]For a recommended definition of "equities" and further comment on the accounting implications of this term, see
pp. 181-183 of this chapter.

collection of homogeneous "rights," inclusion therein of a "right" that is not attended by a contribution of capital is not to be recommended. By such inclusion, a party represented as realizing an infinite return on investment[1] would be permitted to distort the aggregate return on investment of those parties who <u>do</u> provide some capital.[2]

The Greer article precipitated an exchange of letters between Paton, Greer, and Carman Blough.[3] Paton contended that "net profit in its basic and most useful meaning signifies net to those who invest money in the enterprise. . . .[4] Describing Greer's recommendation as "rather unrealistic and unwise strategically,"[5] Paton nonetheless recognizes the persuasiveness of Greer's view that the government, in effect, participates as a partner with stockholders. Notwithstanding this argument, however, he maintained his position that

---

[1]In reality, the "return to the government," if such a measure possesses any significance at all, is of course less than infinity; its measurement requires a quantification of the value of the resources committed to each enterprise through the medium of government operations. At present, this value is incapable of being computed--in practice or in concept.

[2]For general agreement that the government is not an equity-holder except "under a broad social concept of the corporation," see Eldon S. Hendriksen, "The Treatment of Income Taxes by the 1957 AAA Statement," The Accounting Review, XXXIII, No. 2 (April, 1958), p. 217.

[3]The contents of the two letters between Greer and Blough, being only tangentially related to the issue at hand, are not referred to in the following commentary.

[4]"The Accounting Exchange," The Accounting Review, XXI, No. 1 (January, 1946), p. 86.

[5]Ibid.

income taxes are a pre-net income deduction " in view of the
fact that the government makes no investment and that we still
have private enterprise after a fashion, and also in view of
the fact that taxes are a coerced payment prescribed by statute. . . ."[1]

Greer's reply[2] unveiled a new approach: the manager
(for whom the statements are prepared)[3] is responsible for
the administration of the enterprise assets--to the extent
that he can exercise control over their destinies. He is not
accountable for the way in which the capital was financed or
(by the same token) the manner in which the profit is to be
distributed. Income taxes being coerced and dependent (largely)
on the existence of accountants' net income, (1) the manager
has no control over such an expenditure,[4] and (2) the income
tax obligation is a claim against net income and therefore
relates to "financial administration," not to "property util-

---

[1]Ibid.   [2]Ibid., pp. 86-87.

[3]It should not necessarily be inferred from this statement that managers are the most important recipients of financial statements; as will be pointed out below, one or more
groups of capital suppliers are the major recipients. It appears to be Greer's view that all capital suppliers (including
short-term trade creditors) are the relevant group, although
he recognizes that managers, of necessity, will also utilize
the financial statements. More specifically, it is the entire
group of capital suppliers who will assess the effectiveness
of management.

[4]Li disagrees: "Income taxes, as a cost, are subject
to managerial control and reduction as other costs are." Li,
"Income Taxes and Income Tax Allocation under the Entity Concept," op. cit., p. 268.

ization."[1]

"I am not inclined to disagree materially with much of anything you say," concedes Paton in response.[2] He further states that full-fledged managerial control over assets is probably a thing of the past, anyway:

> A business enterprise operates in a structure of technological and institutional arrangements and factors and its particular status in the tax structure, for example, is just as much a part of its environment as its particular status in its relation to the labor market, transportation, or some other factor.[3]

Furthermore, if the final return to owners is unsatisfactory, there is no reason to obscure the true nature of the progress of the enterprise by drawing a balance prior to deducting high taxes, concludes Paton.

The argument that income taxes are a distribution of net income because they are calculated on the basis of net

---

[1]Ironically, Greer employs a distinction that earlier received expression in the Paton and Littleton monograph, which was published at a time when Paton still contended that income taxes were properly a distribution of net income. Hence, Greer utilizes a Patonian argument (developed when Paton would have agreed with Greer on the income-tax argument) in attempting to defeat Paton's new thesis. The Paton-Littleton distinction was between "asset utilization" and "equity administration." W. A. Paton and A. C. Littleton, An Introduction to Corporate Accounting Standards (Chicago: American Accounting Association, 1940), Monograph No. 3, p. 100; see also p. 102, ibid., for specific reference to income taxes (quoted below, p. 168 and footnote 1). Paton today seems to accept this dichotomy as valid, but he would classify income taxes under "asset administration."

[2]"The Accounting Exchange," op. cit., p. 87.

[3]Ibid., p. 88.

income[1] evoked the following comment from Montgomery: "It is true that federal taxes are based on 'net income,' but the taxes are based on net income before federal taxes--the net income which remains after taxes is the true net income of the business."[2]

The Committee on Accounting Procedure of the American Institute of Certified Public Accountants (then the American Institute of Accountants), inaugurating its drive for the general acceptance of intra-period and inter-period tax allocation, announced in 1944 that "income taxes are an expense which should be allocated, when necessary and practicable, to income and other accounts, as other expenses are allocated."[3] In a later paragraph, the Committee somewhat relaxed its prescription, stating that the provision for income taxes "may be included at the end of the income statement, immediately preceding the showing of net income for the period, or it may be appropriately classified as an operating expense."[4] Paton, a

---

[1]More precisely, the amount of the tax is based on "taxable income," not accountant's "net income." Here, they are taken as being roughly the same.

[2]Robert H. Montgomery, Auditing Theory and Practice (New York: The Ronald Press Company, 1927), Fourth Edition, Revised and Enlarged, p. 361.

[3]"Accounting for Income Taxes," Bulletin No. 23 (December, 1944), American Institute of Certified Public Accountants (formerly the American Institute of Accountants), Accounting Research Bulletins, 1-51, prepared by the Committee on Accounting Procedure (New York: American Institute of Certified Public Accountants, 1939-59), pp. 183, 186.

[4]Ibid., p. 184. This position, without the relaxation, was affirmed in 1953: "Restatement and Revision of Accounting Research Bulletins," Bulletin No. 43, loc. cit. (New York, 1953), p. 88.

member of the Committee at that time, assented to the contents of the bulletin. Upon examining the financial statements of several hundred companies' annual reports from 1958 to 1960, this writer noted a significant proportion of income statements that avoid taking a stand on the issue. Their means of avoidance,[1] which the Committee on Terminology of the American Institute of Certified Public Accountants does not seem to discourage,[2] leaves the (official) accounting

---

[1]An improvement, assuming (1) that income taxes are to be deducted as an item separate from other deductions, and (2) that the companies deem income taxes to be a pre-net income item, would be:

     NET INCOME, before deducting income taxes
       Income Taxes
     NET INCOME

The companies would probably take exception to the word, "avoidance," stating that they prefer the use of "net income before deducting income taxes" and "net income after deducting income taxes" in order solely to emphasize the relation of the tax burden to net income--accomplished also by the singling out of "income taxes" as a separate deduction. But which of the two balances is meant to be the net income? A reader of such an income statement cannot tell. The method the companies now use breeds an equivocality that, if the above recommendation were adopted, would be removed without sacrificing any of the desired emphasis.

[2]"Proceeds, Revenue, Income, Profit, and Earnings," Bulletin No. 2, American Institute of Certified Public Accountants (formerly the American Institute of Accountants), Accounting Terminology Bulletins, 1-4, prepared by the Committee on Terminology (New York: American Institute of Certified Public Accountants, 1953-57), (March, 1955), p. 3, para. 8. Accounting Terminology Bulletin No. 4, as noted below, classifies "taxes" as "expense," yet Accounting Terminology Bulletin No. 2, cited above, seems to permit a "net income" before taxes--if it is properly described as such. "Cost, Expense and Loss," op. cit., Bulletin No. 4 (July, 1957), p. 2. It is significant that, in 1944, the Committee on Accounting Procedure reacted as follows: "The committee believes that the term 'net income before income taxes' has unfortunate implications, and urges that the word 'net' be eliminated therefrom." "Accounting for Income Taxes," Accounting Research Bulletins, No. 23, p. 192. This recommendation is in the

stature of income taxes shrouded in equivocality.

Similarly, the position of the Institute with respect
to the orientation postulate and, conjointly, the concept of
income has been somewhat beclouded--although in recent years
its stand has been more clearly and unambiguously stated.
The Institute's position in 1941 is best exemplified by the
following recommended outline of the income statement:[1]

> Sales
> Less cost of sales
> Gross income
> Deduct expenses
> Net income from sales
> Deduct bond interest
> Net income of the corporation
> Preferred dividends
> Net income for common stock

One might infer from the foregoing hierarchical structure
that the "equities-beneficiary" view was being followed, because the first "net income" figure is drawn before deducting interest. The remaining "net incomes" may be accordingly
interpreted as portions of the "net income" applicable to
particular groups. But Bulletin No. 32, issued in 1947,[2] implies that the "proprietor-beneficiary" view is the recommended
practice. The doubt largely disappeared in 1957, when Termin-

---

right direction, but, in this writer's opinion, does not go far
enough. If income taxes are to be treated as an "expense," it
is inconsistent therewith that either an "income" (other than
"gross income") or "net income" should be drawn before deducting said income taxes.

[1]"Report of Committee on Terminology," Accounting Research Bulletins, No. 9 (special) (May, 1941), p. 73.

[2]"Income and Earned Surplus," ibid., No. 32, pp. 259-
67.

ology Bulletin No. 4 stated that the "narrower" interpretation of "expense" includes interest as well as taxes.[1]

Since the promulgation of Accounting Research Bulletin No. 23, in 1944, articles on intra-period and inter-period (mostly the latter in recent years) have pervaded the literature. Advocates of inter-period allocation[2] contend, essentially, that the net income of each period should reflect an income-tax charge that has been causally the result of the revenues and other charges which are algebraically combined to find net income. Clearly, the protagonists' argument, as thus paraphrased, contemplates that income taxes are a pre-net income item. Alternatively, one might argue that allocation is proper in order to show only that portion of the income-tax "distribution" (from net income) which is causally related to the revenues and charges that were algebraically combined to find that net income. Here, income taxes are treated à la Greer. In both cases, an argument can be made to support allocation. (This is not to imply that such an argument is incontrovertible. In the present study, this writer will not declare a position relative to the allocation question.)

---

[1] "Cost, Expense and Loss," op. cit., p. 2. But see footnote 2, p. 160, above.

[2] Henceforth, "allocation," when having reference to tax allocation, will refer to inter-period, rather than intra-period, allocation.

But it seems to this writer that the problem is more urgent when net income itself will be affected by the decision of whether or not to allocate.[1] As already noted, Accounting Research Bulletin No. 23, in first advancing the allocation argument, explicitly classified the income-tax provision as a determinant of net income. Although this writer has essayed no such survey, it would seem a priori that more of those who concur with the Institute's handling of the income-tax provision would also be ardent supporters of allocation as a necessary accounting practice than would be true of those who would place the income-tax provision after the net-income balance. If net income is at all an important figure, tax allocation would be a more crucial problem if the income-tax provision were one of its determinants. Indeed, for some accountants, the entire decision as to whether to allocate at all might turn on the choice of an orientation postulate and, thereby, a concept of net income.[2]

---

[1] Sprouse agrees. See his "The Significance of the Concept of the Corporation in Accounting Analyses," op. cit., p. 377.

[2] "If income taxes were treated as a distribution of income, after the manner of dividends, most of the problems associated with the reporting of income taxes would disappear; in that event the amount of the tax bill, as reflected in the tax return, would be charged directly to retained earnings." Maurice Moonitz, "Income Taxes in Financial Statements," The Accounting Review, XXXII, No. 2 (April, 1957), p. 175. As indicated above, this writer would not necessarily agree with Moonitz' last statement.
"The most convincing case for income tax allocation rests upon its proper matching of expense with revenue. . . ." Willard J. Graham, "Income Tax Allocation," The Accounting Review, XXXIV, No. 1 (January, 1959), p. 15; emphasis supplied.
It is suggestive that among the few accountants who have published dissents from the argument in favor of tax al-

The American Accounting Association, through either
its Executive Committee or its Committee on Concepts and
Standards, since 1936 has vacillated between the proprietor-
beneficiary and equities-beneficiary approaches. In 1957,
it announced its support for the latter as well as the Greer
concept of income taxes:

> The realized net income of an enterprise measures
> its effectiveness as an operating unit and is the
> change in its net assets arising out of (a) the ex-
> cess or deficiency of revenue compared with related
> expired cost and (b) other gains or losses to the
> enterprise from sales, exchanges, or other conver-
> sions of assets. Interest charges, income taxes,
> and true profit-sharing distributions are not deter-
> minants of enterprise net income.
> In determining net income to shareholders, how-
> ever, interest charges, income taxes, profit-sharing
> distributions, and credits or charges arising from
> such events as forgiveness of indebtedness and con-
> tributions are properly included.[1]

---

location, at least Davidson and Hill treat income tax as a
distribution of income. See Perry Mason, Sidney Davidson,
and James S. Schindler, Fundamentals of Accounting (New York:
Henry Holt and Company, 1959), Fourth Edition, p. 287 (in
all substantive respects the same paragraph which appears in
Perry Mason and Sidney Davidson, Fundamentals of Accounting
(Brooklyn: The Foundation Press, Inc., 1953), Third Edition,
p. 168); Sidney Davidson, "Accelerated Depreciation and the
Allocation of Income Taxes," The Accounting Review, XXXIII,
No. 2 (April, 1958), pp. 173-80; and Thomas M. Hill, "Some
Arguments Against the Inter-Period Allocation of Income
Taxes," The Accounting Review, XXXII, No. 3 (July, 1957),
pp. 357-61, especially pp. 357-58.

[1]American Accounting Association, Accounting and Reporting Standards for Corporate Financial Statements and Preceding Statements and Supplements, A Report of the Committee
on Concepts and Standards (Columbus, Ohio: American Accounting Association, 1957), p. 5; emphasis in original. Although
the use of two net incomes dilutes somewhat the applicability
to the 1957 Revision of the entity-subject, equities-beneficiary view, the same argument can be employed here as was
used in connection with the recommended outline of the income
statement contained in Accounting Research Bulletin No. 9
(special); see supra, p. 161.

The Association's stand did not pass unnoticed. Kelley contended that two varieties of net income are "illogical, contrary to common sense and contrary to universal business practice."[1] Net income, according to Kelley, can mean only "net income to stockholders."[2] As one would expect, a proprietor-beneficiary adherent, as is Kelley, would object to the drawing of a "net income" balance before deducting income taxes (and interest). After reviewing the arguments against the deduction of income taxes prior to determining "enterprise net income," Hendriksen, another critic of the Association's position on income taxes, writes as follows:

> Although there are some obvious differences between the calculations of income taxes and other expenses, the similarities in their nature are more basic. Customarily, the classification of an expense is based on the type of benefits received, many of which are quite indirect. Property taxes, for example, must be associated with the specific property used in order to determine the benefits received by the corporation. The benefits of such property cannot be received unless the property tax is paid or recognized as payable. Similarly, the income tax (like a franchise tax) is associated with the right to conduct a profitable corporation in a favorable economic climate. This is certainly a valuable consideration. The fact that the price of this right (the amount of the tax) varies from corporation to corporation does not affect its basic classification in the statements. This classification is independent of the method of calculation. If the amount of the tax were determined by the last two digits of the firm's telephone number,

---

[1] Arthur C. Kelley, "Comments on the 1957 Revision of Corporate Accounting and Reporting Standards," The Accounting Review, XXXIII, No. 2 (April, 1958), p. 214.

[2] Ibid., p. 215.

most accountants would not deny its place among
expenses.[1]

Hendriksen's argument is both cogent and persuasive.
Income taxes are a kind of excise levy for the privilege of
conducting operations in an advantageous economic environment. That the government has chosen "income" as the point
of reference for calculation of the tax is a matter of form
and not of substance.[2] Conceivably any number of other factors could have been selected as the base: gross margin,
square feet of floor space occupied, number of employees,
compensation of officers, and so forth. The use of "income"
ostensibly makes the tax dependent on the taxpayer's ability
to pay. Implicit in the use of "income" is the apparent pre-
sumption that those corporations that reap the greatest profits have, ipso facto, derived the most benefit from the "advantageous economic environment." Hence, ability to pay is
measured by the apparent benefits obtained, and if a corporation pays a tax as the inevitable consequence of being profitable, a calculation of (enterprise)[3] "net income" before
taxes would at best be artificial and factitious. Furthermore, as pointed out above,[4] the government does not invest
funds as do creditors (other than the government in respect

---

[1]Hendriksen, "The Treatment of Income Taxes by the
1957 AAA Statement," op. cit., p. 217.

[2]For agreement, see L1, "Income Taxes and Income Tax
Allocation under the Entity Concept," op. cit., p. 265.

[3]By "enterprise net income" is meant the return to
all capital suppliers.

[4]See pp. 155-156, supra.

of taxes) and stockholders; the government, as a consequence,
does not possess sufficiently similar attributes of typical
equity-holders (that is, investment of funds and assumption
of risk) to warrant a merger of the two parties under the
heading of "equities."[1]

The use of "income" as the basis for the tax calculation should not be allowed to obscure the true nature of
the levy. Had Walter Reuther's profit-sharing plan of 1958[2]
been accepted by the auto industry, would it have followed
ineluctably that that portion of employee compensation which
is tied to profitability be treated as a "distribution of
income"? It is a matter of public record that the high-
ranking officers of many large corporations are voted bonuses
by the directors on the basis of the profitability of the
year's operations.[3] Are these bonuses, therefore, a "distribution of income"? The point of reductio ad absurdum
would be reached very soon as more and more cost factors were
found to have an affinity toward "income."

---

[1]Compare with Hill, "Some Arguments Against the Inter-
Period Allocation of Income Taxes," op. cit., pp. 357-58.

[2]See "Reuther to Seek Share of Profits and Pay Increase," The New York Times, January 14, 1958, pp. 1, 36; and
"Text of Reuther Proposals on Auto Contracts and Companies'
Replies," The New York Times, January 14, 1958, p. 36. Indeed,
some 20,000 enterprises, as of early 1958, were splitting
"profits" with employees. A. H. Raskin, "Reuther's 1958 Model,"
The New York Times, January 15, 1958, p. 26.

[3]See, for example, Dean H. Rosensteel, "Current Trends
in Top Management Compensation," The Management Review, XLVI,
No. 12 (December, 1957), pp. 10-15, especially p. 15.

This writer finds it difficult to accept the statement, made by Paton and Littleton in 1940, that " income taxes . . . are not costs of producing the economic service which accounts for the revenue from sales."[1] On the contrary, income taxes (in the United States, at least) are the cost of establishing and maintaining a free economy within which private enterprise can effectively attempt to attain profitable results. Translated into microeconomic terms, income taxes are thus a cost of a firm's revenues.

Canning: An Economist's View

Utilizing the sole proprietorship as his image of "enterprise," Canning writes:

> The association in speech and writing of liabilities and of net proprietorship [that is, "proprietorship" in the usual sense] as though these two quantities were coordinate and had an independent existence, cannot but be misleading to those who are not fully informed. . . . Then, too, we find writers [Cole and Paton are later cited by Canning as examples] who give a single name to the right-hand member of the balance sheet and treat the items in it as though they were not merely coordinate but homogeneous as well.[2]

Why Canning does not employ the corporation as his "enterprise" illustration is soon made clear: the corporation, according to Canning, is a figure of speech, an "imaginary entity," not a reality. It is a "blunder" to identify the stockholders as the proprietors of the corporation. "The

---

[1] Paton and Littleton, An Introduction to Corporate Accounting Standards, p. 102.

[2] John B. Canning, The Economics of Accountancy: A Critical Analysis of Accounting Theory (New York: The Ronald Press Company, 1929), p. 51.

shareholders, as such, are proprietors of their shares only--
they have mere contracts with the corporation in which certain beneficial interests in the corporation's affairs are
granted. . . ."[1]

To Canning, indeed, the proprietor of corporate enterprise is the corporation itself, for Canning's "proprietor"
is the "asset-holder," or owner of the assets. The stockholders, being owners of the corporation, not of its assets,
are not proprietors (except of their shares). It then follows that the liabilities are the claims against the asset-
holder--not against the enterprise assets. Consequently,
"gross proprietorship" is equal to (that is, identical to)
the assets. The liabilities being claims against the asset-
holder, his net free-estate, or "net proprietorship," is the
excess of the assets over the liabilities. This entire network of interrelationships in Canning's system unfolds like
a series of syllogisms if one only accepts the major premise:
that the proprietor is the asset-holder, or corporation.

The strictly legal overtones of Canning's model are
apparent. By law, the corporation owns the assets, and by
law, the creditors of the enterprise have (first) recourse
against the owner of the enterprise assets. As regards proprietorships and partnerships, the owner or owners of the
firm would also be the asset-holders, or proprietors. "Gross
proprietorship" would still be equal (and be identical to)
the assets, and the "net proprietorship"--in no way related

[1] Ibid., p. 55.

to the net worth _items_ commonly found in the balance sheet
(it is only an _amount_, not divisible into invested capital
and undistributed profits)--is the numerical difference between the value of the assets and the amount of the liabilities. In Canning's words:

> Net proprietorship . . . does not literally im-
> ply either: (1) an overstatement of assets (elsewhere
> in the statement); or (2) an identity with capital
> instruments; or (3) a positive opinion about the cap-
> italized value of the enterprise; or (4) a coordinate
> footing of proprietor and creditor. It does imply
> that the set of operations in enterprise whereby some
> person (or persons) has become a holder of assets (a
> proprietor) may also have given rise to adverse items.
> It is this algebraic sum of interests of the proprietor
> that the term 'net proprietorship' is intended to de-
> scribe.[1]

At first inspection, what begins as a criticism of
the Patonian entity-subject, equities-beneficiary view seems
to have come full circle, for one would expect Canning to say
next that net income should be related to "gross proprietorship." But one may well ask how Canning effects a connection
between the asset-holder-corporation and the stockholders.
The latter are completely outside of the Canning static[2] model.

---

[1] _Ibid._, p. 54. For further discussion of this somewhat
abstract point, see chap. 4, _ibid._

[2] The term "static" is appropriate because Canning, in
the discussion referred to, is developing an analysis in balance-sheet, or positional, terms. Similarly, the comparing of
successive balance sheets would be an exercise in "comparative
statics." An income-statement analysis, being couched in terms
of changes over time, is referred to herein as a "dynamic" approach. It is perforce true that the income statement will
yield the same final difference as will a comparison of the beginning and ending balance sheets, yet the income statement is
intrinsically a report of change; consequently, it may conveniently be referred to as a dynamic instrument.

If net income is defined with reference to "gross proprietorship," in what manner (which is explainable in the context of his static model) is any portion of that net income
filtered down to the stockholders--so as to identify a "net
income to stockholders"? The answer is clear: there is no
way.

Canning then proceeds to develop the outlines, albeit
vaguely drawn, of a dynamic model--in order to propound a
concept of income. Relying very heavily (indeed, almost exclusively) on the writings of Irving Fisher, Canning appears
to settle on a concept which attaches, or relates, "income"
to stockholders,[1] but nowhere does he say this in such explicit and unambiguous terms that would fully convince this
writer. Canning writes, for instance:

> When the accountant prepares an income statement
> for a private business enterprise, he describes the
> extent to which past activities in the enterprise
> have enhanced the ability of those beneficially in-
> terested [that is, the stockholders, for a corpora-
> tion] in the proprietorship to command future final
> income.[2]

Elsewhere, he writes: "The accountant is concerned with income as it emerges in enterprise relations; he undertakes to
show to whom the beneficial interest in income runs. . . ."[3]
But he states at another point: "The accountant's procedure

---

[1] See ibid., pp. 161, 169-70. Canning's meaning is
quite difficult to discern, for the author seldom uses "normative" words such as "should" or "ought." When he says that
the accountant "determines" income [in a certain way], does
Canning advocate this approach, or is he merely stating what
appears to him to be a fact?

[2] Ibid., pp. 159-60.   [3] Ibid., p. 91.

in dealing with income is, in some respects, the least satisfactory part of his procedure."[1] No clear-cut amplification
of this latter statement is offered by its author.

Nevertheless, if Canning can be understood to say
that accounting should relate income to the "beneficial interests," it clearly cannot be done within the context of
his static model, if income is first defined in terms of an
annexation to "gross proprietorship." It must be concluded,
therefore, that Canning--in the light of the inferences that
can be drawn from his dynamic model--essentially does not
disturb the proprietor-beneficiary view that Paton attempted
to dismantle.

Chow, after offering a very lucid and discerning re-
construction of the Canning argument, arrives at substantially
the same conclusion:

> We may say that Canning's concept of asset-
> holder is useful in pointing out that there are two
> aspects of asset ownership that should be carefully
> distinguished: the immediate interest--possession,
> control, and disposal of specific assets--and the
> beneficial interest--claim to income and capital,
> unspecified as to asset items. He fails to indicate,
> however, that accounting is concerned only with the
> second aspect, and that that aspect need not have a
> capital value to find accounting expression. We
> may also conclude that his is not an entity theory,
> nor a reconstruction of the proprietorship theory,
> but a mere modification of the latter. He starts
> out with an entity approach [that is, the static
> model], fails to follow through, and ends with an
> ordinary proprietorship view [that is, the dynamic
> model].[2]

---

[1]Ibid., p. 90.

[2]Y. C. Chow, "The Doctrine of Proprietorship," The
Accounting Review, XVII, No. 2 (April, 1942), p. 161. This
writer is indebted to Chow, who, through his article, greatly
clarified Canning's argument.

Although one must acknowledge Canning's unique and thoughtful rearrangement of the balance-sheet, or static, relationships, he nonetheless must conclude that it is non-operational in producing <u>within the system</u> either (1) a hierarchical ranking of returns to different suppliers of assets, or (2) an income to the party ultimately interested in the efficacy of the enterprise. Canning overlooks, in stating his major premise, that the "beneficial interest" consists of those who are assuming the greatest amount of risk--those who have the power (although seldom the inclination) to determine whether the firm shall continue or not. The well-insulated enterprise of his static model does not make provision for a necessary means of financial communication between the enterprise and its capital suppliers. Although the corporation is a means to an end, it is not also the end.

Vatter: "Fund Theory"

The published version of Vatter's doctoral dissertation,[1] which has generated surprisingly little comment in the literature, is an attempt to wed the English double-account form of the balance sheet with the ordinary funds statement. The results are not unlike those of the present-day accounting for institutions and governmental bodies.

The enterprise is divided into any number of "funds"

---

[1] William J. Vatter, The Fund Theory of Accounting and Its Implications for Financial Reports (Chicago: The University of Chicago Press, 1947); the author summarizes his "fund theory" in "Corporate Stock Equities--Part I," in Morton Backer (editor), Handbook of Modern Accounting Theory (New York: Prentice-Hall, Inc., 1955), pp. 367-70.

--the simplest division probably being the twofold breakdown into a "current fund" for current assets and current liabilities and a "capital fund" for fixed assets and all other right-hand items save retained earnings. Financial statements resembling a sectional balance sheet and typical funds statement are used to depict the status, and nature of changes in the residual equity, of each fund.

Each fund is devoid of personalistic attachments. A fund may relate to a particular purpose, activity, or situation. The assets and equities of each fund are viewed, respectively, as service potentials and restrictions thereagainst; in this respect governmental accounting is most closely approximated. The resulting financial statements may be rearranged, quite flexibly, to suit the specific purpose or purposes for which they are being used.[1]

Vatter's system includes no overt attempt at determining an "income." Indeed, the motive power behind Vatter's new mode of financial recapitulation is his dissatisfaction with both the "entity theory" and the "proprietary theory" (as well as with any single concept of "income," which will be discussed below):

> Neither the proprietary theory nor the entity theory is a wholly satisfying frame of reference for accounting. Each is vulnerable in that it adopts a personality as its focus of attention. The difference between them is mostly whether the person (for whom the books are kept and to whom the reports are made) is the 'proprietor' or proprietors in their

---

[1] For a concise summary of the anatomy of his fund accounts and the "theory," see Vatter, Fund Theory, pp. 94-95.

human selves, or whether real people must be viewed abstractly or in the guise of a fictional entity, corporate or otherwise. The weakness in these personalized bases for accounting is that the content of accounting reports will tend to be affected by personal analogies; and issues will be decided not by considering the nature of the problems but upon some extension of personality--to reach or to support conclusions that are for the most part mere expediencies. Dependence upon personality and personal implications in accounting theory, even as a convention, does not contribute to that objectivity toward which all quantitative analysis is aimed.[1]

He argues that "entity" data are no more "managerial" than are "proprietary" data--an obvious reference to Paton's "managerial point of view"--for "Management is concerned fully as much with what ought to be, or with what might have been, as it is with the actual events that occur."[2]

Furthermore, financial data that are oriented toward a personification inevitably fail to meet the needs of the major users of financial statements: management, social control agencies, and actual and prospective creditors and investors.[3] The solution, writes Vatter, is "to abandon entirely the notion of a 'general purpose' income statement and to force a reading of the entire financial report simply by abstaining from any reference or suggestion of an income computation in overt form."[4] The reader must therefore derive for himself a figure, or figures, that will suit his specific purposes. Gone is the general-purpose income figure which, according to Vatter, is practically valueless for application

---

[1]Ibid., p. 7. By his parenthetical phrase, does Vatter assume that the two parties are, of necessity, always the same?

[2]Ibid., p. 35.   [3]Ibid., pp. 8-9.   [4]Ibid., pp. 75-76.

to particular problems.

Vatter's Fund Theory contains a wealth of penetrating criticism of conventional concepts and conventional financial statements. But this writer must agree with Vatter's reviewer[1] who complains that the author presents many more questions than answers. And how many readers of financial statements will have the ability and patience to ferret out the figures that are most useful for them? For a large number of readers it might be more constructive to provide a general-purpose figure, such as income, which, although it may not be the optimal figure in most instances, will nonetheless act as a reference point from which they could estimate a more telling quantum. It is not consistent with the scope and object of the present study to evaluate at length the "fund theory" contribution.

Vatter's criticism of the general-purpose income is nonetheless meritorious, and will be reintroduced for further comment in Chapter VI.

Husband: The "Representative" View

George R. Husband, in a pair of thought-provoking articles,[2] points out what he believes are inconsistencies

---

[1] Eugene C. Moyer, Review of The Fund Theory of Accounting and Its Implications for Financial Reports, by William J. Vatter, The Accounting Review, XXIII, No. 4 (October, 1948), pp. 440-41.

[2] George R. Husband, "The Corporate-Entity Fiction and Accounting Theory," The Accounting Review, XIII, No. 3 (September, 1938), pp. 241-53; and George R. Husband, "The Entity Concept in Accounting," The Accounting Review, XXIX, No. 4 (October, 1954), pp. 552-63.

in the application of the entity-subject, equities-beneficiary[1] point of view--as he interprets it. He cites these
statements of Paton and Littleton as being mutually inconsistent:

> The business undertaking is . . . an entity or
> institution in its own right, separate and distinct
> from the parties who furnish the funds. . . .[2]
> Emphasis on the entity point of view . . . re-
> quires the treatment of business earnings as the in-
> come of the enterprise itself until such time as
> transfer to the individual participants has been
> effected by dividend declaration.[3]
> Between the moment when profit has been earned
> by the enterprise and the moment when profit-assets
> are distributed to investors, those who contributed
> capital have a claim against the assets according
> to their contracts.[4]
> . . . .
> Gains and losses are changes in enterprise assets,
> not in proprietors' assets or in stockholders' assets.[5]

To these views, Husband rejoins as follows:

> To hold that income earned by the corporation
> is not the stockholders' income and to contend that
> the resulting retained earnings are their equity is
> to take the position . . . that some mystical trans-
> formation takes place between income and retained
> earnings which converts nonstockholder income into
> stockholders' equity. That any such mystical trans-

---

[1]Husband's criticisms apply with equal force to the
entity-subject, proprietor-beneficiary point of view.

[2]Paton and Littleton, An Introduction to Corporate
Accounting Standards, p. 8.

[3]Ibid.

[4]Ibid.; emphasis supplied. In the light of the Paton-
Littleton argument, already noted (see p. 168, supra), that
taxes are not a deduction in arriving at net income, how can
the authors justify the inclusion of taxes among the claims of
"equity-holders"? The excerpt cited by this footnote does not
permit it, for the government (1) does not contribute capital,
and (2) has no contractual claim to the firm's assets.

[5]Ibid., p. 9.

formation actually takes place is seriously to be
doubted. If the view that corporate income is entity income and not stockholder income be accepted,
the following conclusions would appear to be inevitable: (1) that the resulting retained earnings
are entity equity; and (2) that the giving to the
stockholders of specific rights thereto through the
medium of a stock dividend constitutes income to
the stockholders.[1]

Undistributed profits of a corporation, according to
Husband's interpretation of the entity-subject view, are the
"corporation's proprietary equity in itself."[2] Nonetheless,
by some kind of metaphysical operation, he contends that
stockholders' invested capital, by the entity-subject view,
is "stockholders' equity." Retained earnings are therefore
the "entity's equity" and stockholders' investment is "stockholders' equity." Consequently, a common-on-common stock
dividend would be interpreted by believers in the entity-
subject view as an income-producing transaction to the stockholders, for they will thereby realize an increase in "their"
equity. Similarly, "book value per share" must exclude undistributed profits for the latter are not a part of "stockholders' equity"--they are yet an equity of the corporation-
entity. This Canning-like construct is thus represented as
the entity-subject view's ramifications on the results of
the accounting process.

As an alternative view which is "a more realistic
basis for the development of accounting principles," the

---

[1]Husband, "The Entity Concept in Accounting," op.
cit., pp. 555-56.

[2]Ibid., p. 554. See related discussion, pp. 122-126
of Chapter IV.

"representative" approach[1] is urged by Husband. In order to make clear Husband's reasons for advocacy of this latter view, the following lengthy excerpt is reproduced:

> Considerable tendency exists in current account-
> ing to relate basic theory to the presumption that
> the corporation as an entity conducts its affairs
> for its own ends [compare this comment with the fi-
> nal remarks, above, in connection with the implica-
> tions of the Canning static model]. Basic account-
> ing problems are solved in a manner more or less
> consistent therewith. From the point of view of
> economics, however, the core principals in free en-
> terprise activity are the individual entrepreneurs
> who use the various forms of business organization
> for personal ends. It is they who keep free enter-
> prise society on its feet by assuming the ultimate
> responsibility for business conduct. Their desire
> for profit is the motivating force underlying the
> formation, the continued operation, and the expan-
> sion and contraction of business. Free enterprise
> will remain free only as long as its entrepreneurs
> function efficiently and they will function effi-
> ciently only as long as profits, or the prospect of
> profits, possess the appearance of adequacy. 'En-
> trepreneurial' profit, or the prospect of such prof-
> it, is therefore the key factor in the efficient
> functioning of free enterprise society. The primary
> goal of accounting is the measurement of this prof-
> it. By so doing it indicates the efficiency with
> which the respective free enterprise endeavors func-
> tion and provides the best possible base for estima-
> ting prospective future profits. Since the locus of
> the entrepreneurial function rests in personal indi-
> viduals rather than in impersonal business entity it
> would appear that accounting theory would be more
> realistically hinged to economic reality if the cor-
> poration were assumed to be an agency organization.
> From the economic point of view the solution of
> many accounting problems would in turn appear to be

---

[1]The "representative" approach holds that the proprietor owns all of the business assets and owes all of the business liabilities. In effect, it is the same as Hatfield's conception of the "proprietary theory": in terms of its accounting
results, it is almost identical to that of the entity-subject,
proprietor-beneficiary view. The only difference between the
latter and the "representative" approach is that advocates of
the "representative" approach insist that the proprietor owns
the business assets and owes the business liabilities. See p.
126 of Chapter IV, supra. Husband also refers to his approach
by the terms "association" and "agency."

more realistic.[1]

Clearly, the entity-subject view, as envisaged by Husband
(and by Canning in his static model), does not lend much importance to the role of individuals; the corporation is seen
as both the "means" and the "end" from the accounting point
of view. Consequently, from Husband's recitation of the
properties of the entity-subject view and its implications
for accounting theory, one is inclined to turn to the "representative" approach as the only effective means of achieving
a kind of accounting that is consistent with pre-eminence, as
argued by Husband, of the individual economic actor.

But, as Husband points out, the conventional accounting interpretation of transactions that involve the stockholder are no more in harmony with the "representative" view
than with the entity-subject view. For example, the "representative" view would have income accrue to the stockholders
as soon as it accrues to the corporation; therefore, a cash
dividend would be properly interpreted as a return of capital
--in effect, an anticlimactic event. But it is not so viewed
in practice, nor is a stock dividend generally regarded as a
transfer of income to the stockholders,[2] nor does a book-value

---

[1]Husband, "The Entity Concept in Accounting," op. cit.,
pp. 553-54.

[2]On the question of the nature of a stock dividend,
compare Edward B. Wilcox, "Accounting for Stock Dividends: A
Dissent from Current Recommended Practice," The Journal of
Accountancy, XCVI, No. 2 (August, 1953), pp. 176-81; with
James T. S. Porterfield, "Dividends, Dilution, and Delusion,"
Harvard Business Review, XXXVII, No. 6 (November-December,
1959), pp. 56-61.

computation ignore the existence of retained earnings. In the face of this disharmony, Husband's conclusion is somewhat perplexing:

> While for different purposes it is desirable that items being analyzed be treated in a manner relative to the purpose at hand, published statements are best set forth from the 'entrepreneurial' point of view.[1]

In effect, he seems to say, "the ends justify the means, but accountants should steer as closely as possible to the 'representative' point of view. This is how the market interprets such transactions."

That these alleged inconsistencies exist may be due to Husband's manner of interpreting the entity-subject view. True, the enterprise is "separate and distinct" from its capital suppliers. But it is circular to say that the corporation has "an equity in itself," as it is circular to say that treasury stock is an asset.[2] Undistributed profits of the entity may be an equity in its assets, but not in itself. And what is meant by "equity"? Paton, who first used the term in an accounting context, is the appropriate source.

---

[1] Husband, "The Entity Concept in Accounting," op. cit., p. 563.

[2] Indeed, Husband agrees that treasury stock is not an asset. "[Treasury stock] should not be carried as an asset." George R. Husband and Olin E. Thomas, Principles of Accounting (Boston: Houghton Mifflin Company, 1935), p. 385; in the latter quotation, the authors indicate that it is only a general principle, suggesting the possibility of exceptions. But in 1949: "Logically . . . it is difficult to justify a position which results in presenting the corporation as a stockholder in itself." George R. Husband and William J. Schlatter, Introductory Accounting (New York: Pitman Publishing Corporation, 1949), p. 312.

In his Accounting Theory, equities are "claims," "rights,"
or "interests" in the assets, or the "distribution of ownership" in the assets.[1] Paton must not mean "legal ownership,"
else the definition of "equities" would be different for incorporated enterprises than for unincorporated organizations
--and his equities-beneficiary view is meant to apply, with
possible exceptions, to all kinds of firms.[2] Could he mean
"right" in the sense of "right to control" or "right to exact
services from"? This possibility must be rejected, for
"stockholders' equity" in the assets--particularly for the
large, publicly-held corporation--would not imply a right to
control the assets. The following paragraph from Theory,
however, yields the answer:

> Equities, as a practical matter, must be stated
> in terms of properties as of a given date. The
> present interests may be such as to have a right to
> all the future earnings of the business; but it is
> only as such earnings are realized, that is, reach
> a condition where they are capable of definite
> statistical expression in terms of current properties,
> that they can be reflected in the equities.[3]

(It should be noted that this Patonian conception of "equities"
--as opposed to that which stresses the control over assets--
concurs with the position taken by Chow.)[4] "Equities" are
therefore--in the equities-beneficiary sense--rights to future
earnings (as well as to existing assets). They are long-run

---

[1]Paton, Accounting Theory, pp. 37-42.

[2]See pp. 135-139 in Chapter IV, supra.

[3]Paton, Theory, p. 42; emphasis in original.

[4]See p. 172, supra.

rights, evidencing a beneficial interest. When the profit-
assets are severed from the entity by formal action, the
beneficial interest becomes an actual or realized interest--
the interest has matured. These equities, consistent with
the equities-beneficiary view, are divided among creditors
and stockholders. (Within the "stockholders' equity" section,
the nature of the subdivisions is influenced strongly, and
quite properly so, by the stipulations of the various corporation statutes.)[1] In the framework of this interpretation
of the nature of "equities," the "inconsistencies" posed by
Husband quickly dissipate. Book-value properly includes all
of "stockholders' equity"; cash dividends are a distribution
of income, but, logically, not until payment has been made;
and stock dividends are merely structural shiftings within
the "stockholders' equity" section. "Equities," so viewed,
are a reflection against the backdrop of ownership and cred-
itorship of the beneficiary interest in the entity's assets.

Were Husband's undefined "entity's equity in itself"
carried to its logical conclusion, the effort would be self-
defeating. The so-called liabilities must logically also be
the "entity's equity in itself." There appears to be no way,

---

[1]For a discussion of the interrelationships of accounting and legal principles in connection with the "stockholders' equity" section, see Robert T. Sprouse, "Accounting
Principles and Corporation Statutes," The Accounting Review,
XXXV, No. 2 (April, 1960), pp. 246-57. Paton and Paton dissent somewhat from usual accounting practice by preferring
to merge in one account the "par amount" and "excess over
par" received from stockholders. William A. Paton and William A. Paton, Jr., Corporation Accounts and Statements (New
York: The Macmillan Company, 1955), chap. 3.

save the aforementioned "metaphysical operation," to credit
to the "entity's equity in itself" the entity's income when
it is not also recognized that the entity has an equity in
the assets which have generated that income. Husband's balance sheet thus reduces to a list of assets and their values
set in opposition to the "entity's equity in itself," equal
in amount to the total value of the assets. Such a balance
sheet, it is hardly necessary to add, would be of little use
beyond what could be learned by examining the composition
and values of the assets.

Husband's advocacy of the primacy to accountants of
the interest of the residual equity-holders--a proposition
that demands careful attention--is not affected by the defeat
of his "bill of inconsistencies." In order to accept as valid
Husband's emphasis for accounting purposes on the interests
of residual equity-holders, one need not embrace the view
that "they own all the business assets and owe all the business liabilities." As will be argued in Chapter VI, the manner in which all, or any group, of capital suppliers may be
singled out for primary emphasis in the entity-subject income
statement depends on the figure which is labeled "net income."

Staubus: The Institutional-Entity Approach

What is the entity's point of view? "Obviously,"
writes George J. Staubus, "the entity will try to protect its
own interest."[1] Its goal is to retain as much of its revenues

---

[1]George J. Staubus, "Payments for the Use of Capital
and the Matching Process," The Accounting Review, XXVII, No. 1
(January, 1952), p. 105.

as possible. Consequently, "income" to the entity is the increase in retained earnings.

But what factors would motivate the managers of the
entity? Staubus offers three possibilities: (1) the needs
of the voting equity, (2) the perpetuation ("growth and continuity") of the entity, and (3)--if the managers are also
owners--a high return to the manager-owners. Possibilities
(1) and (3) have a proprietary viewpoint. Only possibility
(2) approximates the entity viewpoint of retained earnings
maximization. Thus, if Paton did not intend to arrive at
proprietary-oriented accounting results, his "managerial point
of view" must have been that of possibility (2). "Income" to
the managers--if "proprietary-theory" results are to be avoided
--must consequently be the increase in retained earnings.
(Note that Staubus unquestioningly identifies the "entity
theory" solely with Paton's "managerial point of view," implying that both, of necessity, call for a "return to all equities." To Staubus, the entity-subject, proprietor-beneficiary
alternative is apparently not an available choice, except insofar as he would characterize the "proprietary theory" as
yielding results that are identical to those that derive from
the former.[1] For the reason that underlies Staubus' neglect
of the entity-subject, proprietor-beneficiary alternative, see
below.)

This construct naturally requires that interest be
viewed as an expense rather than as a distribution of income.

---

[1]See p. 126 of Chapter IV, supra.

In this regard, he attempts to strike an analogy between interest and two common items of expense: wages and rent. Endeavoring to draw them together, so as to justify the inclusion of interest among the expenses, he argues:

> The fact that equity holders often contribute their services under a long term contract while employees usually can withhold their services and terminate the relationship at any time does not seem to be an important distinction for the present purpose. The fact that employees take their 'stores of services' home every night while investors leave theirs in the possession of the corporation continuously until they decide to withdraw (usually by transferring their interests to new equity holders) is important for some purposes but not for deciding what is income to a corporation.[1]

After noting that whether an enterprise rents a building or borrows money in order to buy the building, it is nonetheless paying for the use of money, he adds:

> . . . Interest paid by the owner of a mortgaged plant building should be given very nearly the same accounting treatment as would rent on that building if the contract for the use of it took the form of a lease, e. g., as overhead charged to work in process inventory in a manufacturing plant. Using the terminology of Paton and Littleton, interest cost attaches to other costs in the same way that labor cost and overhead attach. Likewise, interest cost expires when its contribution to revenue is realized. In theory there is no good reason why the basic concepts of 'cost,' 'costs attach,' and 'matching costs and revenue' should not be applied to interest cost as they are to other costs.[2]

Staubus then proceeds to ascertain the "asset interest rate" (that is, explicit interest and dividends divided

---

[1]Staubus, op. cit., p. 108. Staubus' argument appears to be sketchy; consequently, his conclusions are hardly conclusive.

[2]Ibid.; footnote omitted. Why should interest "be given very nearly the same accounting treatment"? How close must two sets of facts be to each other in order that each should be accounted for in "very nearly" the same way?

by average assets). He then capitalizes the "explicit interest and dividends" by applying the rate to all of the
asset values so as to effectuate the matching of revenues
and causally-related costs (whether they are connected with
the "physical" production of revenues or not).

It is of interest that Staubus, in a later article,[1]
announces his loyalty to the "residual equity point of view"
(that is, entity-subject, proprietor-beneficiary) as opposed
to his construction of the "entity theory." His reasons for
choosing the residual equity point of view do not warrant
recapitulation here.

The difference between the Patonian version of the
"entity theory" and that of Staubus is traceable to a disagreement over the meaning of the word "entity." Staubus,
in conceiving an orientation that would be consistent with
"entity theory," apparently concluded that by "entity" is
meant that the managers or, if one will permit, the entity,
are the parties at interest. It is for them that financial
statements are prepared. This conception might be termed
the "entity-subject, entity-beneficiary view"; again, the
entity is seen as both the means and the end of economic
activity. But, as noted above, Paton's "managerial point of
view" suggests only that the managers' performance in utilizing the "given" assets should be judged apart from their
success in raising funds by various means; by his "entity

---

[1]George J. Staubus, "The Residual Equity Point of
View in Accounting," The Accounting Review, XXXIV, No. 1
(January, 1959), pp. 3-13.

view," or "managerial point of view," Paton does not establish either the managers or the entity as the dominant[1] beneficiary of financial accounting data. Thus, the objective of the managers--be it "growth and continuity" or otherwise--is of no consequence to the "entity view" as enunciated by Paton and others. Staubus' construction of the "entity view" might therefore be called the "institutional-entity view," leading to the shorthand expression, entity-subject, entity-beneficiary. Paton's, on the other hand, might be called the "distributional-entity view," leading to either "entity-subject, proprietor-beneficiary" or "entity-subject, equities-beneficiary"; Paton chooses the latter. As will be shown below, Nammer and Suojanen (the former only for part of his analysis) also employ the "institutional-entity view." In assessing the value of their arguments, it is therefore desirable to keep in mind these two broad approaches to the meaning of "entity": institutional, wherein the interests of the managers (and the entity) are paramount; and distributional, wherein the interests of one or more groups of capital suppliers are paramount.

Nammer: An Activity Concept

Helmi M. Nammer, in a doctoral dissertation at the

---

[1]Paton, in fact, establishes the capital suppliers as the dominant parties at interest. That they are only "dominant" and not the sole parties at interest is important: the managers are also involved. See the related discussion in Chapter IV, supra.

University of Illinois,[1] replaces the proprietary and entity
points of view by his "activity concept." His reformulation
calls for the reporting of two income figures--"operating
income" and "owners' income," although these terms are not
used in their usual senses. His objective is to find an
orientation postulate that should be applied to all kinds
of enterprise and that is consistent with the nature of
modern enterprise.

Nammer begins by questioning the profit-maximization
goal ascribed to the firm by the classical economists. After
examining some criticisms of the present-day applicability of
marginal analysis, he concludes that "survival and growth"--
long-term goals--is the most acceptable conception of the
objectives of (large) business enterprise today.[2]

He then proceeds to criticize the "proprietary theory"
as (1) placing too much stress on a personality, the owners;
(2) being inconsistent with the continuity assumption; (3)
being inapplicable to the corporate form; and (4) being too
short-term (for example, he interprets the "proprietary theory"
as regarding the assets mainly as debt-paying media) to produce results which are in harmony with the "survival and
growth" objectives of enterprise.

---

[1]Helmi Mahmoud Nammer, "An Activity Concept of the
Business Enterprise and Its Implications in Accounting Theory"
(unpublished Ph.D. dissertation, Graduate College, University
of Illinois, 1957); abstract reproduced in James S. Schindler
(editor), "Abstracts of Dissertations in Accounting," The
Accounting Review, XXXIV, No. 4 (October, 1959), pp. 622-23.

[2]Nammer, op. cit., chap. 4.

The "entity theory" is criticized for (1) placing too much stress on a personality, the management; (2) being inapplicable to the unincorporated firm; and (3) being too short-term to produce the desired long-term results. Nammer then advances an "activity concept" as being usable for all kinds of business organizations and as meeting present-day legal and economic requirements:

> The activity concept is based on the idea that a business organization is a complex system of formal and informal coordinated activities for the purpose of creation or transformation and distribution of utilities. This definition emphasizes two functions of a business organization. First, as a productive economic entity it has the function of creation or transformation of utilities (production or exchange of goods and services). The emphasis here is on the idea that a business organization is separate and distinct from the participants. It is the activities rather than the individuals who contribute these activities which are important for accomplishment of the organization objective. Second, as a method of doing business for the participants, the business organization serves the function of distribution of utilities. The emphasis here is on the individual participants who are willing to contribute their activities in order to satisfy their personal aim. Therefore, the activity concept makes it possible to join together the view that the business enterprise is a separate entity and the view that it is also an association of individuals.[1]

Because of his postulated objectives of business enterprise, Nammer concludes that the true owners are all long-term capital suppliers; they have the "residual beneficial interest." His balance-sheet equation is therefore:

Assets - Short-term Liabilities = Net Worth + Long-term Liabilities[2]

He argues, like Vatter, that present-day income figures are

---

[1]Ibid., p. 153. [2]Ibid., pp. 165-68.

oriented toward either the owners or to management—always
to a personification:

> In order to arrive at a definition of income
> that emphasizes all the basic attributes of income,
> and that is useful for owners as well as management,
> one must avoid any personification in income defi-
> nition. Rather, the emphasis should be on the view-
> point of the business enterprise; this is the essence
> of the activity concept.[1]

(Untrue to his statement of principle, and unlike Vatter, he
regards favorably an "owners' income," or the return to long-
term capital suppliers.)

Nammer then proposes the use of two net incomes.
"Operating income" represents essentially the current-operating concept of income, before deducting taxes, gains and
losses from the settlement of short-term liabilities, gains
and losses from the sale or exchange of assets, gains arising
from gifts and donations, bond interest, and dividends.[2]
"Owners' income"—owners being all long-term capital suppliers
—is found by deducting from "operating income" the first
three items, above. He does not compute a return to stockholders alone.

Nammer's accounting results, it should be noted, reflect no radical valuation concepts; he is concerned mainly
about which balances in the income statement should be emphasized. One may question whether any one-year income measure
is a significant and valid clue to the long-run efficacy of
enterprise activities—for it is "survival and growth" which
he wishes to measure. But the criticism of Nammer's analysis

---

[1]Ibid., p. 170.   [2]Ibid., p. 180.

will not be grounded in this point.

Nammer's attempt to relate the activities of the accounting unit to long-term capital suppliers suggests roughly the same degree of concern on the part of all such capital suppliers for the "survival and growth" of the firm. It would seem, however, that the aspirations toward success of the accounting unit of different long-term capital suppliers might vary greatly. Bondholders are restricted by a contractual limitation on their return. The character of the return to preferred stockholders differs from that of the return to common stockholders. Those who take the ultimate risk, the common stockholders, are grouped--for purposes of ascertaining the "residual" income--with those whose risk is substantially less and whose claim is legally enforceable irrespective of (1) whether there are "profits" out of which to pay the return, and (2) whether management wishes to give them their share.

There is good reason for calculating a return to all capital suppliers, or even all long-term capital suppliers-- but not on the grounds that such an amount represents "residual" equity, or that it necessarily measures the long-term efficacy of enterprise operations. Viewed in a different light, Nammer's "owners' income," which seems to be identical to Paton's net income,[1] has the merit of calling attention to

---

[1] As noted above, Paton would exclude current liabilities from the group of "capital suppliers" to which a net income may be related. See Paton, Theory, pp. 260-64; and footnote 2, pp. 98-99, supra. In concept, it nonetheless seems that a fully logical application of the Patonian construct would

a measure of management's success in administering the assets
with which it has been provided, regardless of the method of
financing those assets. A measure that gauges management's
effectiveness in utilizing all of its assets would seem to
provide a useful starting point from which to determine
whether expansion or contraction of the asset base, again
without regard to the means of financing, would be desirable.
A measure such as Nammer's "owners' income" or Paton's net
income would, when compared with such balances as "return to
preferred and common stockholders" and "return to common stockholders," permit management (and the stockholders who might
wish to evaluate management's decision) to decide upon the
most profitable (to the common equity) method of financing
these assets. Nammer's breakdown, however, does not readily
furnish all of this information.

It should be recalled that regardless of how strongly
one regards the enterprise as the accounting unit, enterprise
activity is undertaken ultimately for the benefit of individuals. And it is individuals--as owners, creditors, or man-
agers--who make business decisions. Although it may be true
that "survival and growth" are uppermost in the minds of management, it does not necessarily follow that these objectives
are as cherished by every capital supplier. Insistence on a
single measure of business success, say, Nammer's "operating
income," may have applicability to only a limited number of

include in "capital suppliers" (and thus in the group to
which "net income" is related) all amounts owing that are
not paid as soon as the legal liability matures.

income-statement readers--principally members of management. Although Nammer seems to share Vatter's view[1] that "income" has been overemphasized as the measure pre-eminent, he none-theless prefers to strike two income figures. And the second (and final) balance, "owners' income," is oriented toward long-term capital suppliers, whose legal and economic roles are nonhomogeneous; hence, the balance--as a "residuum"--has only ambiguous reference to any one relatively homo-geneous group of long-term capital suppliers. It is true that they have committed long-term funds (directly or in-directly) to the enterprise, but it is also true that they need not maintain a long-term relationship to the enterprise --they may dispose of their interests in one of many securi-ties markets. The longer-run loyalties to the enterprise, it would seem, are those of the management whose mobility of labor service is presumably much less, on the average, than the capital suppliers' mobility of capital.

The role of Nammer's "operating income" is more ques-tionable, in the light of the author's proclivities toward a long-run analysis. If Nammer is truly interested in a long-run measure, why stress a balance which--because of its "current-operating" characteristic--is unaffected by inter-period corrections and adjustments? Such insulation from the consequences of uncertain estimates of prior periods (resulting in the current period, as one instance, in a gain or loss on the sale of assets) is not consistent with a long-

---

[1]Vatter, Fund Theory, pp. 7-8, 75-76.

run view of income measures: one year's figure, being tentative and a matter of judgment,[1] is but one in a series of such figures in the firm's history. And Nammer's treatment of taxes--as a deduction from "operating income" and therefore as a "non-operating" charge--is, to say the least, enigmatic. Finally, Nammer's quest for a single "theory" to be applied to all enterprises is, as will be pointed out in Chapter VI, a misdirected objective.

It will be noted also, in the light of the discussion in the previous section, that Nammer is working at cross-purposes. At the same time he is attempting to resolve "institutional" and "distributional" objectives; the result is a hodgepodge that satisfies neither.

Suojanen: The Enterprise Theory

"As the enterprise is studied," writes Waino W. Suojanen, "it becomes apparent that many decisions are made in which the interests of the stockholders are not paramount."[2] Suojanen concludes that for the large, publicly-held corporation today, survival and growth overshadow the "predatory"

---

[1] Writes May: "They are accounts of happenings in a world of business which is subject to constant and sometimes violent change and full of uncertainties; naturally, they cannot rise higher in the scale of certainty than the events which they reflect." George O. May, "Improvement in Financial Accounts," in Dickinson Lectures in Accounting (Cambridge, Mass.: Harvard University Press, 1943) p. 47 (paper read as the Dickinson Lecture in Accounting, at the Harvard University Graduate School of Business Administration, Cambridge, Mass., 1937).

[2] Waino W. Suojanen, "Accounting Theory and the Large Corporation," The Accounting Review, XXIX, No. 3 (July, 1954), p. 394.

quest for maximized profit. Social property rights command
the attention of corporate managers more so than do "nominal"
private property rights (of the stockholders). The "organization objective" is strongly influenced by social responsibilities. If it were not, more government controls would
be forthcoming. Ergo, the enterprise is most fruitfully
examined from its societal perspective. A "value-added" type
of analysis, similar to that which was the cornerstone of the
now-laid-aside input-output matrix at the national level, is
advanced as a plausible society-oriented approach.

The Suojanen proposal may have real merit, in addition

Although he finds that both the proprietary and entity
"theories" are outdated for large, publicly-held corporations,
Suojanen nevertheless retains the customary income statement,
relegating the value-added analysis to status as a supplemen-
tary report. Unless this recommendation is a concession to
the practical difficulties of instituting change, Suojanen
apparently sees some value in the present income statement.

The Suojanen proposal may have real merit, in addition
to being a contribution toward resuscitating the national
input-output system of accounts. Retention of the income
statement, moreover, is commendable. Notwithstanding their
tendency toward awareness of social responsibilities, large
corporations are nevertheless profit-conscious. Attention
to social duties would seem to presuppose the existence of an
adequate cushion of profit, else corporations might find agi-
tated stockholders at their doors. Suojanen seems to say that
an all-out pursuit of profit, almost irrespective of the
methods (if lawful) used, may incur the wrath of society, via

additional government regulation. Indeed, large corporations
may find it strategically wiser to follow a socially-acceptable
path to higher profits--that is, both goals are possible of
attainment, after a concession from each. This is not the
place to develop a theory of corporate behavior, but one who
discerns a modicum of restraint in the corporate zeal for
profits should not rush to conclude[1] that "survival, growth,
and attention to social responsibilities" are relevant and
profit is irrelevant. Because the two sets of objectives
appear to compete for managerial attention, a package of (at
least)[2] the income statement and value-added statement contains two useful tools of analysis.

Suojanen, it should be noted, is concerned solely
with the "institutional-entity view."

Bedford: A Residual Equity Approach

Norton M. Bedford describes the difference between
the "proprietary theory" and "entity theory" as reducing to
a question of beneficiary, not subject.[3] To Bedford, the
"proprietary theory" is what this writer calls the entity-
subject, proprietor-beneficiary view. The "entity theory,"

---

[1]This is not to imply that Suojanen is among those
who choose one extreme or the other; he seems to recognize
the presence of some of each.

[2]Included also would be the balance sheet, and, if
useful in the circumstances, the funds statement. The income
statement has been singled out only because of its relevance
to the Suojanen thesis.

[3]Norton Moore Bedford, "A Critical Analysis of Accounting Concepts of Income" (unpublished Ph.D. dissertation,
Graduate School, The Ohio State University, 1950).

on the other hand, is the Patonian conception: entity-subject, equities-beneficiary.

In order to reconcile the difference, Bedford proposes seven groups for whom income might be reported:[1]

1. The economic entity
2. The total original creditor and stock equity group
3. The total remaining original creditor and stock equity group
4. The total original stock equity group
5. The total remaining original stock equity group
6. The total original junior stock equity group
7. The total remaining original junior stock equity group.

After relatively brief discussion of each possibility, he concludes as follows:

> The income of the total remaining original junior stock equity group should be reported, for it is this group or members of this group for whom managements endeavor to provide an income. A measure of managerial efficiency would be reflected by using this concept. Also reporting the income accruing to this group would not preclude reporting the income accruing to other groups in the same income report. It would thus be possible to report the income of the economic entity, deduct certain charges to determine the income accruing to the total original stock equity group, and other deductions would follow to arrive at the income accruing to the total junior stock equity group.[2]

Unfortunately, the latter excerpt is not only circular but is inconclusive. How many incomes should there be? And regardless which of the seven possibilities was chosen, its selection "would not preclude" the striking of a balance for each of the other six.

Bedford is apparently impressed by the voting power

---

ibid.

[1]Ibid., p. 227; for related discussion, see chap. 5, ibid.

[2]Ibid., p. 230; also see p. 89, ibid.

of the common stockholders, although such writers as Nammer
and Suojanen[1] have largely ignored its influence. Though
this writer might accept a number of Bedford's conclusions,
the latter attends too perfunctorily (and in a somewhat un-
incisive way) to the development of a body of logic by which
to clinch his argument.

Bedford makes another point deserving of comment:

> While accountants have not announced it as such,
> the reported 'net operating income' tends to have
> some similarity to the income of the economic entity.
> However, it is not entirely true for gains on sale of
> fixed assets are excluded from 'net operating income'
> and must be included as income accruing to the econ-
> omic entity.[2]

An examination of a number of introductory accounting texts
proves the verity of this statement.[3] Many writers draw a
balance prior to deducting nonrecurring gains and losses,
interest and dividend revenue, interest charges, and dividend

---

[1]For the views of Nammer and Suojanen, see this chapter, supra.

[2]Bedford, op. cit., p. 84. That it has not been so
announced is not altogether clear. "Income and Earned Surplus,"
Accounting Research Bulletin No. 32, op. cit., albeit in an
oblique manner, may be viewed as a kind of such "announcement."

[3]See, for example: Billy E. Goetz and Frederick E.
Klein, Accounting in Action: Its Meaning for Management
(Boston: Houghton Mifflin Company, 1960), chap. 7; Robert R.
Milroy and Robert E. Walden, Accounting Theory and Practice--
Introductory (Boston: Houghton Mifflin Company, 1960), pp.
204-05; George R. Husband, Accounting--Administrative and Fin-
ancial (Philadelphia: Chilton Company, 1960), chap. 4; C. Aub-
rey Smith and Jim G. Ashburne, Financial and Administrative
Accounting (New York: McGraw-Hill Book Company, Inc., 1960),
Second Edition, chap. 5; and William W. Pyle and John Arch
White, Fundamental Accounting Principles (Homewood, Ill.:
Richard D. Irwin, Inc., 1959), Revised Edition, chap. 11.

declarations. This figure is ostensibly designed to portray the "income" of the typical activities of the enterprise, as they relate to its primary function. Interest and dividend items, being "financial" or ancillary, are itemized "below the line." Providing (1) the nonrecurring gains and losses are not material, and (2) interest and dividend revenue are not material, this "net operating income" is a very close cousin to Paton's net income. As Bedford observes, however, it does not appear to be the intent of these writers to derive a "return to all capital suppliers."

Summary[1] and Conclusions

Clearly, the above critical survey of recent literature does not evince a lack of new ideas. Regrettably, however, the innovations have attracted relatively little evaluative response and even less serious consideration for practical application.

For the accounting staffs of regulatory agencies, finance executives, internal revenue agents, securities analysts, and other possessors of a measure of accounting expertise, Vatter's "fund theory"--as applied to external reporting--would seem to have its greatest appeal.[2] The Suojanen model, on the other hand, would appear likely to attract the sympathetic interest of economists.

---

[1] The "summary" portion will omit reference to the discussion on income taxes.

[2] The potential of the "fund theory" for internal reporting is much greater.

It is evident that the word "entity" has been subject to different interpretations. The "entity view" that Paton adopted inquires not at all into the economic self-interest motives of the managers. Rather, it (1) provides capital suppliers with a figure that will gauge their total composite return, and (2) furnishes residual equity-holders a measure of management's effectiveness in asset utilization, irrespective of the manner in which the assets were financed. The Staubus and Suojanen interpretations, stressing the singular importance of the enterprise goals, are thus representative of the "institutional-entity view." Paton's is a "distributional-entity view." The reasons for favoring the latter approach will become evident in Chapter VI.

Until the level of accounting knowledge of the general public increases appreciably, accountants—as the practitioners of an immensely utilitarian discipline—must avoid the use of esoteric analyses. For the short-term future, accountants should attempt mainly to clarify existing principles, procedures, and methods of presentation—within the extant framework. For the longer run, as McCormick has suggested,[1] accountants must embark upon a re-evaluation of the existing structure in order to achieve a more effective communication of financial information to the readers of financial statements. A means of disseminating a greater amount

---

[1]Edward T. McCormick, "Reporting to Stockholders," The Accounting Review, XXXV, No. 2 (April, 1960), pp. 223-27. McCormick is president of the American Stock Exchange.

of knowledge of accounting principles and procedures in-
heres in the long-run problem. The success with which
accountants review and reconstruct the present system may
well depend in large part on the performance of the newly-
constituted Accounting Principles Board of the American
Institute of Certified Public Accountants.

It will be the task of Chapter VI to recommend a
concept of income--consistent with a recommendation as to
the orientation postulate--that will best serve the requirements, for the short-term future, of modern financial reporting.

CHAPTER VI

A REVIEW OF DIFFICULTIES IN THE SELECTION OF
AN ORIENTATION POSTULATE; CONCLUDING
ARGUMENTS AND RECOMMENDATIONS

It is the purpose of this chapter to (1) indicate
the major factors that have tended to obscure the different
conceptions of the orientation postulate, and (2) propose
a general solution. Because a number of the following points
have been developed previously in this study, references to
sources of ideas, having been made in earlier chapters, will
not always be repeated in this summarizing chapter.

Point of View: "Institutional" or "Distributional"?

An important explanation for the variety of orientation postulates—often hazily defined—is the stated or implied assumption of accounting writers that the financial
statements are primarily reports to either management or
capital suppliers. Staubus and Suojanen,[1] choosing the former, represent what might be called the "institutional-entity"
school. Paton,[2] taking the latter, is a member of the "distributional-entity" school. Each position has merit.

---

[1] See Chapter V, supra.

[2] See Chapter IV, supra.

But management is doing much more than apprizing itself of its effectiveness. In Littleton's words:

> Financial statements are sometimes described as reports of managerial stewardship. The last phrase suggests responsibility and duty. . . .
> The direct and primary responsibility . . . is fiduciary and fiscal--the responsibility of an agent possessing property but not owning it. Business managers (of corporations at least) are fiscal agents of other people. . . .
> As enterprise operators they have a duty to operate and to report on operations, that is, a duty to augment as well as protect the owner's property.[1]

To accountants, indeed, the financial statements are representations of the management, not of the auditors _to_ the management.[2] Presumably, little public interest would be involved--and the necessity of _independent_ audits could be avoided--if management were reporting only to itself. To be sure, if such were true, the issue of "independence" (of external auditors from their clients)--so important today[3]--could be safely ignored.

---

[1] A. C. Littleton, Structure of Accounting Theory (Urbana, Ill.: American Accounting Association, 1953), Monograph No. 5, p. 79.

[2] See, for example, The American Institute of Accountants, "Codification of Statements on Auditing Procedure," Statements on Accounting Procedure, based on statements 1 to 24 (1939 to 1949), issued by the Committee on Auditing Procedure (New York: American Institute of Certified Public Accountants, 1951), pp. 8-13.

[3] See Edward B. Wilcox, "Professional Standards," in Robert L. Kane, Jr. (editor), CPA Handbook (2 vols.; New York: American Institute of Accountants, 1952), Volume I, pp. 8-11 of chap. 13; "Proposed Rule on Independence," in "News Report," The Journal of Accountancy, CX, No. 5 (November, 1960), p. 11; and "CPAs Talk of Tougher Rules," Business Week, October 8, 1960, pp. 132, 134.

Management, operating in a trusteeship capacity, is
without question reporting to outsiders, and those outsiders
who possess the most direct financial interest in the enterprise are its creditors and owners. Consequently, the "distributional-entity" view is to be preferred over the "institutional-entity" view.

Point of View: Legal or Economic?

Also of significance in tending to obscure the nature
of the orientation postulate have been the differences between
income-tax and other legal principles on the one hand and
"accounting principles" on the other. It has already been
argued that accounting is concerned preponderantly with economic phenomena, although legal principles will usually play
an important part in specifying the precise nature of the
interrelationships among relevant parties. But accounting
is not a means of legal expression. As George D. Bailey,
past president of the American Institute of Certified Public
Accountants, has said:

> Accounting has considered its own logic and its
> own concepts as of greater importance than statutory
> permissions or requirements. It has adopted the
> consolidated statement of earnings for a parent and
> its subsidiary companies, in spite of the lack of
> legal support; it has its own concepts for distin-
> guishing between earnings and capital; and, finally,
> it has emphasized fairness of presentation of earn-
> ings to avoid misleading inferences instead of a
> legal concept of earnings.[1]

---

[1] George D. Bailey, "Concepts of Income," Harvard
Business Review, XXVI, No. 6 (November, 1948), p. 690 (paper
read as a part of the Dickinson Lecture in Accounting, at
the Harvard University Graduate School of Business Administration, Cambridge, Mass., 1948). Bailey also states that

Accountants have been entrusted with the responsibility for supervising the dissemination of certain types of financial data to outside parties. They may be held liable to their clients or to third parties for various degrees of negligence in discharging the audit function.[1] As a consequence, they must be allowed the latitude to select their own methods--apart from the ways in which government agencies and legal tribunals might determine are best in the light of how they utilize financial reports.

Determination of the "Dominant" Beneficiary in the Case of the Large Corporation

Probably the most influential cause of the multitude of different conceptions of the orientation postulate is the existence of diverse notions of the nature of business enterprise, particularly large corporations. The modern corporation has not become a static institution; it is constantly changing and can today be found, as it were, in all shapes and sizes. Inextricably related to this circumstance is the question of who is the dominant personality for whom accounting reports should be prepared. Is there one dominant personality? If there is, should he be viewed as the only beneficiary of accounting reports? Many decision-makers might conceivably utilize some or all of the data in financial

there is no reason why accountants need to adopt rules solely because they are used for income-tax purposes. Ibid., pp. 687-90.

[1] See Saul Levy, Accountants' Legal Responsibility (New York: American Institute of Accountants, 1954), especially chaps. 1-4.

statements: managers, common stockholders, preferred stockholders, bondholders, short-term creditors, prospective creditors and stockholders, employees, labor organizations, state
and federal regulatory agencies, courts of law and equity,
trade associations, legislatures, economic researchers, stock
exchanges, financial analysts, and taxing authorities, among
many others--and each group may have a multiplicity of purposes in using these data. Should one group be preferred over
the remainder? Yet can all interested parties be satisfied
by a single set of financial reports--such as those that are
contained in the typical annual report of a "listed" corporation? Inevitably, the questions raised in this paragraph
alone vitally affect each of the two orientation subpostulates.
Vatter would divide the enterprise into "funds." Suojanen
would view the enterprise in its societal context. Nammer
would envisage the enterprise as the locus of activities that
are directed toward the twin goals of survival and growth.[1]

One must agree with Vatter that the importance of
"income"--however it is calculated--has been seriously over-
stated. But there is no immediately available means of avoid-
ing the selection of one or more indices of enterprise success.[2] Vatter's "fund" approach may be an acceptable answer,
but it will require--as would any major restructuring--a meth-
odical and purposeful initiation into, first, accounting lit-

---

[1]For a discussion of these writers' views, see Chapter
V, supra.

[2]For this writer's general recommendations to apply to
the longer term, see "Summary and Conclusions" in Chapter V,
supra.

erature, and, second, accounting reports. The "fund theory" is still in incubation, although fourteen years have passed since its birth. At the very least, it must be discussed, developed, and adapted to specific business situations before its usefulness can be fully appreciated. This study will consequently be concerned with the need for a relatively short-term, or temporary, solution. The term "income" being imbedded in accounting literature and financial reports, its use can hardly be avoided as a part of a near-term recommendation. Nevertheless, it should not be employed indiscriminately.

In order to accommodate the selection of the figure that most deserves the appellation "income," it is first necessary to clarify certain relationships, namely, those that exist between the corporation-entity and its individual capital suppliers. Husband puts the point well:

> . . . In a free enterprise society it is the entrepreneur who generates economic activity [;] he is motivated by the prospect of profit, and [therefore] it should be the accountant's basic goal to indicate the entrepreneur's success in this respect. Regardless of the characteristics which the law gives to the corporate form of organization, it remains an organization of individuals. Basically, it is the common stockholders who constitute the entrepreneurs in the case of the corporation and who use it for the purpose of obtaining profit. The final decisions are theirs; they bear the ultimate risk. . . .Accounting comes closest to reality and to being of economic service . . . when it measures 'entrepreneurial' success or failure, and when it imputes profit or loss to the 'entrepreneurial' actors. In so doing it is most consistent with the requirements of free enterprise society.[1]

---

[1]George R. Husband, "The Entity Concept in Accounting," The Accounting Review, XXIX, No. 4 (October, 1954), p. 558. Also see the discussion of Husband's views in Chapter

To Husband's conclusion that common stockholders are the ones
to whom the financial statements should be directed, Schumpeter
would probably take exception. To the latter, the entrepre-
neur--the one who effects new combinations of resources, as
opposed to the "mere manager" who is content with re-using
old combinations in the "circular flow" of economic life--
is the promoter of the enterprise, although he may later become more permanently associated with the organization.[1]
Without entrepreneur-generated "innovation"[2] the economy would
lapse into a statical circular flow, in which the revenues
would exactly cover the return to land and labor; interest,

V, supra. To agree with Husband's conclusions as to the role
of the "entrepreneur," one need not be restricted to his
"representative" viewpoint of the enterprise.

    In regard to Husband's discussion of the role of the
"entrepreneur-stockholder," it matters not that organized
groups (such as investment funds), rather than solely individuals, are financially interested in a given business enterprise. These groups must similarly report to the parties
who have financial interests in them, until, finally, the results of business enterprise as a whole are reduced to the
least common denominator of individuals.

    [1]This synoptic overview of the Schumpeterian analysis
is drawn largely from Joseph A. Schumpeter (translated from
the German by Redvers Opie), The Theory of Economic Development: An Inquiry into Profits, Capital, Credit, Interest, and
the Business Cycle (Cambridge, Mass.: Harvard University Press,
1934); chaps. 2, 3, and 4, and to a lesser extent, chap. 1,
are the most relevant to the present discussion.

    [2]"Innovation" is a technical term meaning the carrying
out of new combinations, for example, new products and new
marketing techniques. "Innovation" means much more than "in-
vention." The former requires that new ideas be made economically operational; the latter does not. For discussion on
this point, see Joseph A. Schumpeter, Business Cycles: A
Theoretical, Historical, and Statistical Analysis of the Capitalist Process (2 vols.; New York: McGraw-Hill Book Company,
Inc., 1939), I, pp. 84-102.

saving, and investment would be nonexistent. Schumpeter's
innovation launches a disequilibrated rhythm from which
"entrepreneurial profit" may emerge. The existence of innovation is thus the explanation of "entrepreneurial profit."
According to Schumpeter, capitalists, who may be creditors
or stockholders, bear the entire financial risk. "Risk-
taking is in no case an element of the entrepreneurial function."[1] In the period of disequilibrium, the excess of revenue over the combined return to land and labor--that is,
"entrepreneurial profit"--is parceled out by the entrepreneur
to the capitalists as their "return"; any portion remaining
after capitalists have been compensated resides with the entrepreneur as his financial reward.

Schumpeter's conception appears to be an important
and valid explanation of enterprise profits; consequently,
it would be desirable to interconnect the accounting concept
of "income" with that of Schumpeter--if an "income" measure
in accord with the latter is accepted as a sound calibrator
of business success. But the Schumpeterian concept of "entrepreneurial profit" becomes very elusive at the practical
level. In large corporations,[2] which executive man-hours are

---

[1]Schumpeter, The Theory of Economic Development, p.
137. The entrepreneur risks only his reputation.

[2]Schumpeter's innovation exists not only in new enterprises. Large corporations having sizable research and
development staffs account for a substantial portion of innovation today. See Jacob Schmookler, "Technological Progress
and the Modern American Corporation," in Edward S. Mason
(editor), The Corporation in Modern Society (Cambridge, Mass.:
Harvard University Press, 1960), pp. 141-65, especially pp.
146-50.

representative of true entrepreneurial activity and which
are merely hours of "labor" in the Schumpeterian sense? No
true profit accrues as a result of the latter. Also, some
capitalists (that is, creditors and, for the most part, preferred stockholders)[1] are to receive only contractually-
limited returns[2]--insensitive to all but the most adverse
conditions. Only the return to common stockholders is (1)
measurable, and (2) not contractually fixed. It would appear,
therefore, that the return to common stockholders is the most
reliable indicator--that is calculable--of the success of
entrepreneurial activity. In this respect, the implications
for practical application of Schumpeter's conclusions would
seem to concur with those of Husband.

Furthermore, it should not be forgotten that the com-

---

[1]See Arthur Stone Dewing, The Financial Policy of Corporations (2 vols.; New York: The Ronald Press Company, 1953),
I, chap. 6. With the exception of "participation" contracts,
the magnitude of the return to preferred stock is almost always fixed. This writer, in studying the properties of "listed" American preferred stocks four years ago, found that
those having "participation" features constituted approximately
2 per cent of all of those listed; consequently, preferred
stocks will be assumed not to have "participation" privileges.

[2]For creditors, "return" means the actual "charge"
recorded in the accounts. In the case of preferred stockholders whose claims are cumulative, "return" includes the con-
tractually-stipulated addition to the accumulated amount. For
non-cumulative preferred stock, "return" means the dividend
declared. For common stockholders, "return" refers to the remainder of the revenues after deducting all costs properly
chargeable thereagainst, as well as the "returns" to creditors
and preferred stockholders. It is important to note that the
"return" to common stockholders does not refer to the dividends
declared or paid on the common shares.

mon stockholder is the largest and ultimate risk-taker. That
Schumpeter's entrepreneurs are the major active forces in
business enterprise should not be allowed to obscure the fact
that such enterprisers cannot operate without capitalists--
and vice versa. As the ultimate risk-takers, common stockholders have exposed themselves to the loss of their investment in consideration of the expectation that they might have
the right to partake, not subject to a stipulated maximum, of
the superabundant fruits of enterprise.[1] Other claimants to
the gains of enterprise rank ahead of common stockholders in
priority, but their demands are limited by contract; accordingly, the assessed risk of these prior claimants, because
their claims are prior and because in the instance of creditors their claims are legally exercisable in the absence of
"profitable" operations, is less than that of common stockholders. Corporation executives (some of whom are true entrepreneurs) are compensated by complex salary, bonus, and stock-
option arrangements, which, although the findings of several
studies are inconclusive,[2] appear to have--at best--only an

---

[1]It should be understood that common stockholders may
"partake" either in the form of dividends or in the form of
price appreciation of their shares.

[2]Arch Patton, in a recent study, finds "no consistent
relationship" between the high compensation of top executives
at the beginning of a six-year period and the trend during the
six years of profits. Other studies covering longer time
spans, he writes, have found better correlations. Arch Patton,
"Trends in Executive Compensation," Harvard Business Review,
XXXVIII, No. 5 (September-October, 1960), p. 150. For the year
1959, Patton finds that 57 per cent of the variation in top-
executive compensation is accounted for by differences in company sales, and that 50 per cent of the variation is explainable by changes in company profits. He concludes that sales

213

imperfect relation to accounting profits. The return to
creditors is contractually set and is usually not discretionary. The return to preferred stockholders is, in theory,
discretionary, but in practice it is usually handled as though
it were mandatory; typically, the return has a fixed upper
limit.[1] Common stockholders participate in the residuum.
Because the magnitude of their return is the most sensitive
of all to the vicissitudes of enterprise success, their natural mindfulness of swings in business activity warrants their
return--if any return is to be so classified--to be singled
out as "income" (preferably called "net income"). Their stake
in enterprise success, as among capital suppliers, is the most
critical; theirs is the most unpredictable.

This writer acknowledges the arguments of writers such

---

are the better yardstick. Ibid.
Roberts finds that sales (that is, size of the firm),
far more than dollar profit, account for the differences between firms in executive compensation. David R. Roberts,
Executive Compensation (Glencoe, Ill.: The Free Press, 1959),
pp. 50-83; see his interesting discussion on pp. 95-108.
Roberts, again using correlation techniques, finds that changes over time in executive compensation show almost identical
relationships to both changes in sales and in profit. Ibid.,
pp. 83-89. Temporally, executive compensation shows far fewer
gyrations than do both sales and profit. Ibid., pp. 25-28.
But Roberts admits that such factors as intangible rewards and
stock options are imponderables that may have real effect on
true executive compensation. Ibid., pp. 89-95, et passim.
See the recent edition of Business Week's annual study on executive compensation: "Top Pay Resists Slump," Business Week,
May 20, 1961, p. 63ff.

[1]Dewing, loc. cit. Also see Benjamin Graham and David
L. Dodd, Security Analysis--Principles and Technique (New York:
McGraw-Hill Book Company, Inc., 1951), Third Edition, pp. 77,
281-82, 352-61. It is significant that Graham and Dodd include the discussion of preferred stocks under the general
heading of "Fixed-Income Securities."

as Berle and Means[1] and Dale,[2] who contend that almost all
stockholders in large, publicly-held corporations have become impotent in controlling the activities of their mana-
gers--except in cases of serious mismanagement. But the
stockholder is no less an interested party; it is only that
he responds in a different way. If the stockholder of today
cannot cause the commotion in the councils of management that
he could fifty and seventy-five years ago, he can nonetheless
expect to find a broader and better organized market for his
securities, should he wish to sell. The stockholder's usual
reaction today is to buy or sell shares, rather than attempt
to influence directly managerial actions. And trading in
securities requires no less an insight into one's "residual"
position than did the more direct means of affecting management decisions some decades ago.

"Net income," therefore, is best used to describe
the return to the residual equity.[3] Nevertheless, the Paton-

---

[1] See Adolph A. Berle, Jr., and Gardiner C. Means,
The Modern Corporation and Private Property (New York: Com-
merce Clearing House, Inc., 1932). Two more recent books by
Berle are: The 20th Century Capitalist Revolution (New York:
Harcourt, Brace and Company, 1954), and Power Without Property:
A New Development in American Political Economy (New York:
Harcourt, Brace and Company, 1959). See also Berle's "Fore-
word" in Mason, op. cit., pp. ix-xv.

[2] Ernest Dale, "Management Must Be Made Accountable,"
Harvard Business Review, XXXVIII, No. 2 (March-April, 1960),
pp. 49-59.

[3] Paton, it would seem, agrees with much of what has
been said in this chapter. Together with his son, he writes:
"The corporate entity becomes a rather empty abstraction unless its activities are viewed through the eyes of some group
or interest. And under present legal and administrative conditions the stockholders represent the corporate membership

ian emphasis on "return to all capital suppliers" deserves a
special place in the income statement. Hatfield's assessment[1]
of the Patonian innovation is correct, but, as Hatfield asserts,
the "return to all capital suppliers" should not be labeled as
"net income."

"Net income" may therefore be defined as that portion
of the "return to all capital suppliers" that inures to the
residual equity.

For the above reasons, the income statement should
specify the "return to all capital suppliers," "return to
preferred and common stockholders," and "return to residual
equity." By this multiple-step arrangement, financial-state-
ment readers can conveniently evaluate the efficacy of the
dual functions of "asset utilization" and "equity administration." A basis for studying the success--past and future--
of "trading on the equity," or "leverage,"[2] is thereby afforded.

---

and the underlying body from which the officers and directors
get their authority and to which they are responsible. The most
generally significant standpoint from which assets and earnings
can be defined is that of the propriety [sic] or stock equity."
William A. Paton and William A. Paton, Jr., Asset Accounting
(New York: The Macmillan Company, 1952), p. 478.
Despite these favorable words for the residual equity
(including, it would seem, the preferred stockholders in cases
where the latter are permitted to vote in the normal course),
Paton nevertheless accords pre-eminence to (that is, labels as
"net income") the "return to (long-term) capital suppliers."
Although Paton occasionally refers elsewhere to the
need for the corporation to be viewed through the eyes of some
"group or interest," his discussion of this point typically
goes no further than does the above extract.

[1]See pp. 145-146 of Chapter IV, supra.

[2]See, for example, Merwin H. Waterman, "Trading on the
Equity," in Wilford J. Eiteman (editor), Essays on Business
Finance (Ann Arbor, Mich.: Masterco Press, 1957), pp. 90-113.

But such a recommendation does not dismiss the more crucial
and fundamental questions: Is the customary income statement
an effective means of portraying enterprise success? Are
there more effectual data-accumulation and data-reporting
approaches? Is present-day financial accounting optimally
suited to a modern corporate society? The foregoing recommendations, being avowedly for the short-term future, implicitly accept the existing accounting structure. Vatter's
"fund theory," among others, demands careful study.

Significance of the Proprietary-Entity Debate

One point remains to be made. The importance of the
controversy over the choice between "proprietary theory" and
"entity theory" has been greatly exaggerated. It was noted
above that some writers envisage the choice of an orientation
postulate as affecting vitally the core of accounting theory.
Some make it appear as though the choice of one approach over
another implies the use of an entirely different concept of
asset valuation--a radical alteration. Such is not the case,
if one works within the existing accounting structure. The
valuation concept need not be affected by a choice of one of
the conventionally available approaches. The problem reduces
to the selection of a balance that deserves the label of "net
income." This decision is important, to be sure, but it is
not nearly so critical as that which these writers attach to
the determination of the orientation postulate.

The problem remains of selecting the appropriate version of the orientation postulate for each accounting situa-

tion. Use of the "distributional-entity" view, together with the consideration mainly of economic (as opposed to purely legal) phenomena, should be followed in making the selection in most cases.

Orientation Problems of Other Kinds of Business Organizations

Most of the preceding discussion in the chapter has been couched in the language and environment of the large, publicly-held corporation. Attention must be devoted also to other forms of enterprise.

The facts of each situation should determine which posture the data-accumulation (first subpostulate) and data-reporting (second subpostulate) processes should assume. The work of the accountant should be designed for the particular situation at hand. Many writers, as noted above, insist that one orientation "theory" must be used for all kinds of enterprise. The jacket must be worn whether it fits or not. This compulsion for universal applicability probably derives in part from the failure to recognize that a postulate rather than a whole body of theory is at immediate issue. Changes in a postulate will not necessarily cause the alteration of any of the remaining theory. This result has been shown to be true of changes in the orientation postulate. In order to arrive at one conception that meets the requirements of all enterprise, these writers run the risk of rising to such a level of abstraction (in order to encompass the major characteristics of the different forms of business organization)

that the chosen conception bears little resemblance to the
facts of many--if not most--of the situations to which it is
supposed to be applied. Moreover, insistence on a reconcil-
iation of economic as well as legal phenomena requires a
result that would be remote from many actual situations.
(As noted many times above, economic factors should predom-
inate.)

Lest it be inferred that this writer advocates that
an enormous inventory of orientation postulates should be
articulated and amassed for application to situations that
differ almost imperceptibly from others, it should be asserted
here that a few postulates will do. This writer's recommendation for large corporations, above, is a kind of compromise
position between the entity-subject, equities-beneficiary and
entity-subject, proprietor-beneficiary views, with somewhat
more stress on the latter. But what approach might be used
for a small firm (be it a corporation or otherwise) that is
owned and operated by the same person? For his purposes, a
full-fledged entity-subject, proprietor-beneficiary approach
may be most effective. Paton's pop vendor at a football game[1]
may best envisage his activities in accord with the proprietor-
subject view.[2] A philanthropic organization might be best
suited for Suojanen's "enterprise" approach. A farmer's ac-

[1]William Andrew Paton, Accounting Theory--With Special
Reference to the Corporate Enterprise (New York: The Ronald
Press Company, 1922), p. 476.

[2]Cf. Stephen Gilman, Accounting Concepts of Profit
(New York: The Ronald Press Company, 1939), p. 53.

counts, or those of the family-owned general store, may call
for application of the economic-citizen-subject view, wherein
the "business" and "household" activities are merged. In
short, the orientation approaches that have been invented
for modern kinds of enterprise do not--solely because they
have been found useful for new modes of enterprise--become
automatically applicable to all, new as well as old, forms
of organization. New approaches are not panaceas because
they are new.

There is also no reason to believe that comparability
among firms is necessarily destroyed by the concurrent use of
several orientation approaches. As has been observed, for
example, the valuation concept--if continuity is assumed--
is as applicable to entity-subject, equities-beneficiary and
entity-subject, proprietor-beneficiary as it is to proprietor-subject.

In sum, accounting postulates owe their existence to
actual experience and fact. Once established, these assumptions should not be permitted to lose contact with reality.

BIBLIOGRAPHY

Books

The American Institute of Accountants. "Codification of
    Statements on Auditing Procedure," Statements on
    Accounting Procedure. A series, based on State-
    ments 1 to 24 (1939 to 1949) issued by the Com-
    mittee on Auditing Procedure New York: American
    Institute of Certified Public Accountants, 1951.

Ballantine, Henry Winthrop. Ballantine on Corporations.
    Revised edition. Chicago: Callaghan and Company,
    1946.

Berle, Adolph A., Jr. Power Without Property: A New Develop-
    ment in American Political Economy. New York: Har-
    court, Brace and Company, 1959.

_____. Studies in the Law of Corporation Finance.
    Chicago: Callaghan and Company, 1928.

_____. The 20th Century Capitalist Revolution. New
    York: Harcourt, Brace and Company, 1954.

Berle, Adolph A., Jr., and Means, Gardiner C. The Modern
    Corporation and Private Property. New York: Commerce
    Clearing House, Inc., 1932.

Black, Homer A., and Champion, John E. Accounting in Business
    Decisions: Theory, Method, and Use. Englewood Cliffs,
    N. J.: Prentice-Hall, Inc., 1961.

Bosland, Chelcie C. Corporate Finance and Regulation. New
    York: The Ronald Press Company, 1949.

Boulding, Kenneth E. Economic Analysis. Third edition.
    New York: Harper & Brothers, 1955.

Brown, Richard. A History of Accounting and Accountants.
    Edinburgh: T. C. & E. C. Jack, 1905.

Canning, John B. The Economics of Accountancy: A Critical
    Analysis of Accounting Theory. New York: The Ronald
    Press Company, 1929.

Churchman, C. West. *Elements of Logic and Formal Science*. Chicago: J. B. Lippincott Company, 1940.

Cole, William Morse. *Accounts--Their Construction and Interpretation*. Revised and enlarged edition. Boston: Houghton Mifflin Company, 1915.

Dewing, Arthur Stone. *The Financial Policy of Corporations*. 2 vols. Fifth edition. New York: The Ronald Press Company, 1953.

Dickinson, Sir Arthur Lowes. *Accounting Practice and Procedure*. New York: The Ronald Press Company, 1918.

Dicksee, Lawrence R. *Advanced Accounting*. Sixth edition. London: Gee & Co., Ltd., 1921.

_____. *Auditing: A Practical Manual for Auditors*. Fourth edition. London: Gee & Co., 1900.

Esquerré, Paul-Joseph. *The Applied Theory of Accounts*. New York: The Ronald Press Company, 1914.

Finney, H. A. *Accounting Principles and Bookkeeping Methods*. 2 vols. New York: Henry Holt and Company, 1924.

Fisher, Irving. *The Nature of Capital and Income*. New York: The Macmillan Company, 1906.

Garcke, Emile, and Fells, J. M. *Factory Accounts, Their Principles and Practice*. London: Crosby, Lockwood and Son, 1887.

Garner, S. Paul. *Evolution of Cost Accounting to 1925*. University, Ala.: University of Alabama Press, 1954.

Gilman, Stephen. *Accounting Concepts of Profit*. New York: The Ronald Press Company, 1939.

_____. *Principles of Accounting*. Chicago: LaSalle Extension University, 1916.

Glynne-Jones, A. *The Companies Acts, 1862 to 1900*. London: Jordan & Sons Limited, 1902.

Goetz, Billy E., and Klein, Frederick E. *Accounting in Action: Its Meaning for Management*. Boston: Houghton Mifflin Company, 1960.

Goode, Richard. *The Corporation Income Tax*. New York: John Wiley & Sons, Inc., 1951.

Graham, Benjamin, and Dodd, David L. Security Analysis--
Principles and Technique. Third edition. New York:
McGraw-Hill Book Company, Inc., 1951.

Gras, N. S. B. Business and Capitalism: An Introduction to
Business History. New York: F. S. Crofts & Co., 1939.

Green, Wilmer L. History and Survey of Accountancy. Brooklyn: Standard Text Press, 1930.

Greer, Howard C. How to Understand Accounting. New York:
The Ronald Press Company, 1928.

Hatfield, Henry Rand. Accounting--Its Principles and Problems.
New York: D. Appleton and Company, 1927.

_____. Modern Accounting: Its Principles and Some of Its
Problems. New York: D. Appleton and Company, 1909.

Hicks, J. R. Value and Capital. Second edition. London:
Oxford University Press, 1946.

Hills, George S. The Law of Accounting and Financial Statements. Boston: Little, Brown and Company, 1957.

Husband, George R. Accounting--Administrative and Financial.
Philadelphia: Chilton Company, 1960.

Husband, George R., and Schlatter, William J. Introductory
Accounting. New York: Pitman Publishing Corporation,
1949.

Husband, George R., and Thomas, Olin E. Principles of Accounting. Boston: Houghton Mifflin Company, 1935.

James, Laylin K. Cases and Materials on Business Associations.
Second edition. Indianapolis: The Bobbs-Merrill Company, Inc., 1949.

Kehl, Donald. Corporate Dividends. New York: The Ronald
Press Company, 1941.

Kester, Roy B. Accounting Theory and Practice. 2 vols.
(First volume is not labeled "Volume I.") New York:
The Ronald Press Company, 1917-18.

Krebs, William S. Outlines of Accounting. New York: Henry
Holt and Company, 1923.

Levy, Saul. Accountants' Legal Responsibility. New York:
American Institute of Accountants, 1954.

Lisle, George. Accounting in Theory and Practice. Edinburgh:
William Green & Sons, 1906.

Littleton, A. C. Accounting Evolution to 1900. New York:
American Institute Publishing Co., Inc., 1933.

_____. Structure of Accounting Theory. Monograph No.
5. Urbana, Ill.: American Accounting Association, 1953.

MacNeal, Kenneth. Truth in Accounting. Philadelphia: University of Pennsylvania Press, 1939.

Marshall, Alfred. Industry and Trade. Fourth edition.
London: Macmillan and Co. Limited, 1923.

_____. Principles of Economics. Eighth edition. New
York: The Macmillan Company, 1948. (This edition was
originally published in 1920.)

Mason, Perry, and Davidson, Sidney. Fundamentals of Accounting. Third edition. Brooklyn: The Foundation Press,
Inc., 1953.

Mason, Perry, Davidson, Sidney, and Schindler, James S.
Fundamentals of Accounting. Fourth edition. New York:
Henry Holt and Company, 1959.

May, George O. Financial Accounting: A Distillation of Experience. New York: The Macmillan Company, 1943.

McLaren, N. Loyall. Annual Reports to Stockholders: Their
Preparation and Interpretation. New York: The Ronald
Press Company, 1947.

Milroy, Robert R., and Walden, Robert E. Accounting Theory
and Practice--Introductory. Boston: Houghton Mifflin
Company, 1960.

Montgomery, Robert H. Auditing Theory and Practice. First
edition. New York: The Ronald Press Company, 1912.

_____. Auditing Theory and Practice. Fourth edition,
revised and enlarged. New York: The Ronald Press
Company, 1927.

Moonitz, Maurice, and Staehling, Charles C. Accounting: An
Analysis of Its Problems. 2 vols. Brooklyn: The
Foundation Press, Inc., 1952.

Newlove, George Hillis, and Garner, S. Paul. Advanced Accounting. 2 vols. Boston: D. C. Heath and Company, 1951.

224

Nussbaum, Frederick L. A History of the Economic Institutions
  of Modern Europe. (An Introduction to Der Moderne
  Kapitalismus, by Werner Sombart, which see.) New York:
  F. S. Crofts & Co., 1933.

Pacioli, Frater Lucas. "De computis et scripturis." (Thirty-
  six chapters from Summa de Arithmetica, Geometria, Proportione et Proportionalita. Venice, 1494.) Translated
  by Pietro Crivelli. An Original Translation of the
  Treatise on Double-Entry Book-Keeping by Frater Lucas
  Pacioli. London: The Institute of Book-Keepers, Ltd.,
  1924.

_____. "De computis et scripturis." (Thirty-six chapters
  from Summa de Arithmetica, Geometria, Proportione et
  Proportionalita. Venice, 1494.) Translated by J. B.
  Geijsbeek. Ancient Double-Entry Bookkeeping. Denver:
  J. B. Geijsbeek, 1914. (Geijsbeek's volume also includes reproductions, notes, and abstracts from the
  works of other writers of the sixteenth and seventeenth
  centuries.)

Paton, W. A. Accounting. New York: The Macmillan Company,
  1924.

_____. Accounting Theory--With Special Reference to
  the Corporate Enterprise. New York: The Ronald Press
  Company, 1922.

_____. Advanced Accounting. New York: The Macmillan
  Company, 1941.

Paton, W. A., and Dixon, Robert L. Essentials of Accounting.
  New York: The Macmillan Company, 1958.

Paton, W. A., and Littleton, A. C. An Introduction to Corporate Accounting Standards. Monograph No. 3.
  Chicago: American Accounting Association, 1940.

Paton, W. A., and Paton, William A., Jr. Asset Accounting.
  New York: The Macmillan Company, 1952.

_____. Corporation Accounts and Statements. New York:
  The Macmillan Company, 1955.

Paton, W. A., and Stevenson, Russell A. Principles of Accounting. Ann Arbor, Mich.: George Wahr, 1917.

_____. Principles of Accounting. New York: The Macmillan
  Company, 1918.

Peragallo, Edward. Origin and Evolution of Double Entry
Bookkeeping. New York: American Institute Publishing Company, 1938.

Pixley, Francis W. Auditors: Their Duties and Responsibilities
under the Companies Acts and Other Acts of Parliament.
Seventh edition. London: Henry Good & Son, 1896.

Pyle, William W., and White, John Arch. Fundamental Accounting Principles. Revised edition. Homewood, Ill.:
Richard D. Irwin, Inc., 1959.

Reiter, Prosper. Profits, Dividends and the Law. New York:
The Ronald Press Company, 1926.

Roberts, David R. Executive Compensation. Glencoe, Ill.:
The Free Press, 1959.

Robertson, H. M. Aspects of the Rise of Economic Individual-
ism: A Criticism of Max Weber and His School. Cambridge,
Eng.: The University Press, 1933.

Robinson, Daniel Sommer. The Principles of Reasoning: An
Introduction to Logic and the Scientific Method.
New York: Appleton-Century-Crofts, Inc., 1947.

Schumpeter, Joseph A. Business Cycles: A Theoretical, Historical, and Statistical Analysis of the Capitalist Process. 2 vols. First edition. New York: McGraw-Hill
Book Company, Inc., 1939.

_____. Capitalism, Socialism, and Democracy. Third
edition. New York: Harper & Brothers, 1950.

_____. The Theory of Economic Development: An Inquiry
into Profits, Capital, Credit, Interest, and the Business
Cycle. Translated by Redvers Opie. Cambridge, Mass.:
Harvard University Press, 1934.

Scott, DR. Theory of Accounts. 2 vols. New York: Henry Holt
and Company, 1925.

Smith, Adam. An Inquiry into the Nature and Causes of the
Wealth of Nations. New York: The Modern Library, 1937.

Smith, C. Aubrey, and Ashburne, Jim G. Financial and Administrative Accounting. Second edition. New York: McGraw-
Hill Book Company, Inc., 1960.

Sombart, Werner. Der Moderne Kapitalismus. 2 vols. Leipzig:
Verlag von Duncker & Humblot, 1902.

Sprague, Charles E. The Philosophy of Accounts. New York:
        Charles E. Sprague, 1907.

Vatter, William J. The Fund Theory of Accounting and Its
        Implications for Financial Reports. Chicago: The
        University of Chicago Press, 1947.

Weber, Max. General Economic History. Translated by Frank
        H. Knight. Glencoe, Ill.: The Free Press, 1927.

Webster's New International Dictionary of the English Language.
        Unabridged. Second edition. Springfield, Mass.:
        G. & C. Merriam Company, 1957.

Wilcox, Clair. Public Policies Toward Business. Chicago:
        Richard D. Irwin, Inc., 1955.

Woolf, Arthur H. A Short History of Accountants and Account-
        ancy. London: Gee & Co., 1912.

Articles and Periodicals

"Abstracts of Dissertations in Accounting." James S. Schindler,
        editor. The Accounting Review, XXXIV, No. 4 (October,
        1959), 612-38.

"Accounting Education," The Journal of Accountancy, CVIII,
        No. 4 (October, 1959), 63-68.

"The Accounting Exchange," The Accounting Review, XXI, No. 1
        (January, 1946), 85-90. (Reproduction of three letters,
        dated June 30, July 5, and July 13, between William A.
        Paton and Howard C. Greer, and of two letters, dated
        July 18 and July 20, between Howard C. Greer and Carman
        G. Blough.)

Alexander, Sidney S. "Income Measurement in A Dynamic Economy,"
        in Five Monographs on Business Income New York: Study
        Group on Business Income of the American Institute of
        Accountants, 1950 , pp. 1-95.

Backer, Morton. "Determination and Measurement of Business
        Income by Accountants," in Handbook of Modern Account-
        ing Theory, ed. Morton Backer; New York: Prentice-
        Hall, Inc., 1955, pp. 207-47.

Bailey, George D. "Concepts of Income," Harvard Business
        Review, XXVI, No. 6 (November, 1948), 680-92. (Paper
        read as a part of the Dickinson Lecture in Accounting,
        at the Harvard University Graduate School of Business
        Administration, Cambridge, Mass., 1948.)

Berle, Adolph A., Jr. "Foreword," in The Corporation in Modern Society, ed. Edward S. Mason. Cambridge, Mass.: Harvard University Press, 1960, pp. ix-xv.

Berle, A. A., Jr., and Means, Gardiner C. "Corporation," in Encyclopaedia of the Social Sciences, ed. Edwin R. A. Seligman and Alvin Johnson. 15 vols. New York: The Macmillan Company, 1930-35, IV, 414-23.

Boursy, Alfred V. "The Name of Paciolo," The Accounting Review, XVIII, No. 3 (July, 1943), 205-09.

Bowers, Russell. "Income Tax and the Natural Person," The Accounting Review, XVI, No. 4 (December, 1941), 358-73.

"CPAs Talk of Tougher Rules," Business Week, October 8, 1960, pp. 132, 134.

Chambers, R. J. "Measurement and Misrepresentation," Management Science, VI, No. 2 (January, 1960), 141-48.

Chow, Y. C. "The Doctrine of Proprietorship," The Accounting Review, XVII, No. 2 (April, 1942), 157-63.

Dale, Ernest. "Management Must Be Made Accountable," Harvard Business Review, XXXVIII, No. 2 (March-April, 1960), 49-59.

Davidson, Sidney. "Accelerated Depreciation and the Allocation of Income Taxes," The Accounting Review, XXXIII, No. 2 (April, 1958), 173-80.

de Roover, Raymond. "The Commercial Revolution of the Thirteenth Century," in Enterprise and Secular Change, ed. Frederic C. Lane and Jelle C. Riemersma. Homewood, Ill.: Richard D. Irwin, Inc., 1953, pp. 80-85.

_____. "New Perspectives on the History of Accounting," The Accounting Review, XXX, No. 3 (July, 1955), 405-20.

Edey, H. C., and Panitpakdi, Prot. "British Company Accounting and the Law, 1844-1900," in Studies in the History of Accounting, ed. A. C. Littleton and B. S. Yamey. Homewood, Ill.: Richard D. Irwin, Inc., 1956, 356-79.

Graham, Willard J. "Income Tax Allocation," The Accounting Review, XXXIV, No. 1 (January, 1959), 14-27. (Paper read before the Annual Meeting of the American Accounting Association, at Syracuse, N. Y., August 27, 1958.)

228

Gras, N. S. B. "Capitalism--Concepts and History," in
    Enterprise and Secular Change, ed. Frederic C. Lane
    and Jelle C. Riemersma. Homewood, Ill.: Richard D.
    Irwin, Inc., 1953, pp. 66-79.

Greer, Howard C. "Treatment of Income Taxes in Corporation
    Income Statements," The Accounting Review, XX, No. 1
    (January, 1945), 96-101.

Hall, C. E. Review of The Evolution of the Science of Book-
    keeping, by H. J. Eldridge, Accounting Research, V,
    No. 4 (October, 1954), 368-69.

Handlin, Oscar, and Handlin, Mary F. "Origins of the American
    Business Corporation," in Enterprise and Secular Change,
    ed. Frederic C. Lane and Jelle C. Riemersma. Homewood,
    Ill.: Richard D. Irwin, Inc., 1953, pp. 102-24.

Hatfield, Henry Rand. "An Historical Defence of Bookkeeping,"
    in Studies in Accounting, ed. W. T. Baxter. London:
    Sweet & Maxwell, Limited, 1950, pp. 1-12.

_____. Review of Accounting, by W. A. Paton, The Journal
    of Accountancy, XL, No. 5 (November, 1925), 389-90.

_____. "What They Say About Depreciation," The Account-
    ing Review, XI, No. 1 (March, 1936), 18-26.

Hendriksen, Eldon S. "The Treatment of Income Taxes by the
    1957 AAA Statement," The Accounting Review, XXXIII,
    No. 2 (April, 1958), 216-21.

Hill, Thomas M. "Some Arguments Against the Inter-Period
    Allocation of Income Taxes," The Accounting Review,
    XXXII, No. 3 (July, 1957), 357-61.

Howard, Stanley E. Review of Principles of Accounting, by
    William Andrew Paton and Russell Alger Stevenson,
    The American Economic Review, IX, No. 3 (September,
    1919), 563-66.

Husband, George R. "The Corporate-Entity Fiction and Account-
    ing Theory," The Accounting Review, XIII, No. 3 (Sep-
    tember, 1938), 241-53.

_____. "The Entity Concept in Accounting," The Account-
    ing Review, XXIX, No. 4 (October, 1954), 552-63.

Kell, Walter G. "Should the Accounting Entity Be Personified?"
    The Accounting Review, XXVIII, No. 1 (January, 1953),
    40-43.

Kelley, Arthur C. "Comments on the 1957 Revision of Corporate
    Accounting and Reporting Standards," The Accounting
    Review, XXXIII, No. 2 (April, 1958), 214-15.

Lane, Frederic C. "Family Partnerships and Joint Ventures in
    the Venetian Republic," in Enterprise and Secular Change,
    ed. Frederic C. Lane and Jelle C. Riemersma. Homewood,
    Ill.: Richard D. Irwin, Inc., 1953, pp. 86-101.

Lawton, W. H. Review of Accounting Theory--With Special Ref-
    erence to the Corporate Enterprise, by William Andrew
    Paton, The Journal of Accountancy, XXXV, No. 4 (April,
    1923), 313-14.

Li, David H. "Income Taxes and Income Tax Allocation under
    the Entity Concept," The Accounting Review, XXXVI,
    No. 2 (April, 1961), 265-68.

_____. "The Nature of Corporate Residual Equity under
    the Entity Concept," The Accounting Review, XXXV, No.
    2 (April, 1960), 258-63.

_____. "The Nature and Treatment of Dividends under the
    Entity Concept," The Accounting Review, XXXV, No. 4
    (October, 1960), 674-79.

Littleton, A. C. "Genealogy for 'Cost or Market,'" The Account-
    ing Review, XVI, No. 2 (June, 1941), 161-67.

Madden, J. T. Review of Accounting, by W. A. Paton, Publica-
    tions of the American Association of University In-
    structors in Accounting, IX, No. 2 (December, 1925),
    158-60.

May, George O. "External Influences Affecting Accounting
    Practice," in Proceedings, International Congress on
    Accounting. New York: [no publisher], 1930), pp.
    686-97. (Paper read before the International Congress
    on Accounting, at New York, September 11, 1929.)

_____. "Improvement in Financial Accounts," in Dickinson
    Lectures in Accounting. Cambridge, Mass.: Harvard
    University Press, 1943. (Paper read as the Dickinson
    Lecture in Accounting, at the Harvard University Grad-
    uate School of Business Administration, Cambridge,
    Mass., 1937.)

McCormick, Edward T. "Reporting to Stockholders," The Account-
    ing Review, XXXV, No. 2 (April, 1960), 223-27. (Paper
    read before the Annual Meeting of the American Account-
    ing Association, at Boulder, Colo., August 26, 1959.)

Moonitz, Maurice. "Income Taxes in Financial Statements,"
    The Accounting Review, XXXII, No. 2 (April, 1957),
    175-83.

Moyer, Eugene C. Review of The Fund Theory of Accounting and
    Its Implications for Financial Reports, by William J.
    Vatter, The Accounting Review, XXIII, No. 4 (October,
    1948), 440-41.

Paton, William A. "Adaptation of the Income Statement to
    Present Conditions," The Journal of Accountancy,
    LXXV, No. 1 (January, 1943), 8-15.

Patton, Arch. "Trends in Executive Compensation," Harvard
    Business Review, XXXVIII, No. 5 (September-October,
    1960), 144-54.

Porterfield, James T. S. "Dividends, Dilution, and Delusion,"
    Harvard Business Review, XXXVII, No. 6 (November-
    December, 1959), 56-61.

"Professional Examinations," The Accounting Review, XXXIV,
    No. 4 (October, 1959), 663-85.

"Proposed Rule on Independence," in "News Report," The Journal
    of Accountancy, CX, No. 5 (November, 1960), 11.

Raskin, A. H. "Reuther's 1958 Model," The New York Times,
    January 15, 1958, p. 26.

"Reuther to Seek Share of Profits and Pay Increase," The New
    York Times, January 14, 1958, pp. 1, 36.

Rosensteel, Dean H. "Current Trends in Top Management Com-
    pensation," The Management Review, XLVI, No. 12
    (December, 1957), 10-15.

Schmookler, Jacob. "Technological Progress and the Modern
    American Corporation," in The Corporation in Modern
    Society, ed. Edward S. Mason. Cambridge, Mass.:
    Harvard University Press, 1960, pp. 141-65.

Solomons, David. "The Historical Development of Costing,"
    in Studies in Costing, ed. David Solomons. London:
    Sweet & Maxwell, Limited, 1952, pp. 1-52.

Sombart, Werner. "Capitalism," in Encyclopaedia of the Social
    Sciences, ed. Edwin R. A. Seligman and Alvin Johnson.
    15 vols. New York: The Macmillan Company, 1930-35, III,
    195-208.

_____. "Medieval and Modern Commercial Enterprise," in Enterprise and Secular Change, ed. Frederic C. Lane and Jelle C. Riemersma. Homewood, Ill.: Richard D. Irwin, Inc., 1953, pp. 25-40.

Sprouse, Robert T. "Accounting Principles and Corporation Statutes," The Accounting Review, XXXV, No. 2 (April, 1960), 246-57.

_____. "The Significance of the Concept of the Corporation in Accounting Analyses," The Accounting Review, XXXII, No. 3 (July, 1957), 369-78.

Staubus, George J. "Payments for the Use of Capital and the Matching Process," The Accounting Review, XXVII, No. 1 (January, 1952), 104-13.

_____. "The Residual Equity Point of View in Accounting," The Accounting Review, XXXIV, No. 1 (January, 1959), 3-13.

Storey, Reed K. "Cash Movements and Periodic Income Determination," The Accounting Review, XXXV, No. 3 (July, 1960), 449-54.

Suojanen, Waino W. "Accounting Theory and the Large Corporation," The Accounting Review, XXIX, No. 3 (July, 1954), 391-98.

Taylor, R. Emmett. "The Name of Pacioli," The Accounting Review, XIX, No. 1 (January, 1944), 69-76.

"Text of Reuther Proposals on Auto Contracts and Companies' Replies," The New York Times, January 14, 1958, p. 36.

"Top Pay Resists Slump," Business Week, May 20, 1961, p. 63ff.

Vance, Lawrence L. "Authority of History in Inventory Valuation," The Accounting Review, XVIII, No. 3 (July, 1943), 219-27.

Vatter, William J. "Corporate Stock Equities--Part I," in Handbook of Modern Accounting Theory, ed. Morton Backer. New York: Prentice-Hall, Inc., 1955, pp. 359-83.

Waterman, Merwin H. "Trading on the Equity," in Essays on Business Finance, ed. Wilford J. Eiteman. Ann Arbor, Mich.: Masterco Press, 1957, pp. 90-113.

Wilcox, Edward B. "Accounting for Stock Dividends: A Dissent from Current Recommended Practice," The Journal of Accountancy, XCVI, No. 2 (August, 1953), 176-81. (The author's first name is incorrectly referred to as "Edmund" on the first page of the article.)

_____. "Professional Standards," in CPA Handbook, ed. Robert L. Kane, Jr. 2 vols. New York: American Institute of Accountants, 1952, I, chap. 13.

Yamey, B. S. "The Functional Development of Double-Entry Bookkeeping," The Accountant, November 2, 1940, pp. 333-42.

_____. "Scientific Bookkeeping and The Rise of Capitalism," in Studies in Accounting, ed. W. T. Baxter. London: Sweet & Maxwell, Limited, 1950, pp. 13-30.

York, Thomas. "Stock and Other Dividends as Income," The Accounting Review, XV, No. 3 (September, 1940), 380-93.

Unpublished Material

Avery, Clarence George. "An Examination of Certain Aspects of Variation Between the Entity Theory and Accounting Practice." Unpublished Master's thesis, Department of Accountancy, University of Illinois, 1956.

Barlow, R. "Medieval Italian Merchants and the Development of Accounting." Unpublished term paper in Business Administration 208, The University of Michigan, May, 1958.

Bedford, Norton Moore. "A Critical Analysis of Accounting Concepts of Income." Unpublished Ph.D. dissertation, Graduate School, The Ohio State University, 1950.

Bodenhamer, Rosa Margaret Brandt. "The Entity Concept of the Firm: A Critical Appraisal." Unpublished Ph.D. dissertation, Graduate School, University of Missouri, 1957.

Kell, Walter Gerry. "The Equities Concept and Its Application to Accounting Theory." Unpublished Ph.D. dissertation, Graduate College, University of Illinois, 1952.

McMoil, William Grove. "An Inquiry into Four Theoretical Concepts of the Corporate Entity and Their Effect upon the Determination of Net Income." Unpublished Master's thesis, Wharton School, University of Pennsylvania, 1958.

Nammer, Helmi Mahmoud. "An Activity Concept of the Business Enterprise and Its Implications in Accounting Theory." Unpublished Ph.D. dissertation, Graduate College, University of Illinois, 1957.

Reports

American Accounting Association. Accounting and Reporting
Standards for Corporate Financial Statements and
Preceding Statements and Supplements. A Report of
the Committee on Accounting Concepts and Standards.
Columbus, Ohio.: American Accounting Association,
1957.

American Institute of Accountants. Changing Concepts of
Business Income. Report of Study Group on Business
Income. New York: The Macmillan Company, 1952.

American Institute of Certified Public Accountants (formerly
the American Institute of Accountants). "Report to
Council of the Special Committee on Research Program,"
The Journal of Accountancy, CVI, No. 6 (December,
1958), 62-68.

Public Documents

U. S. House of Representatives, Subcommittee on Legal and
Monetary Affairs of the Committee on Government
Operations. Hearings, Railroad Accounting Procedures
(Prescribed by the Interstate Commerce Commission).
85th Cong., 1st Sess., April 30, May 1-3, 1957.

Case Citations

Eisner v. Macomber, 252 U. S. 189 (1920).

Hospes v. Northwestern Mfg. & Car Co., 48 Minn. 174 (1892).

Sawyer v. Hoag, 17 Wall. 610 (1873).

Wood v. Dummer, 3 Mason 308, Fed. Cas. No. 17,944 (C.C. Me. 1824).

Published Correspondence

Audits of Corporate Accounts. Correspondence between the
Special Committee on Co-operation with Stock Exchanges
of the American Institute of Accountants and the Committee on Stock List of the New York Stock Exchange,
1932-34. [n.p.]: American Institute of Accountants,
1934.

Other Sources

American Institute of Certified Public Accountants (formerly the American Institute of Accountants). _Accounting Research Bulletins_, 1-51. Prepared by the Committee on Accounting Procedure. New York: American Institute of Certified Public Accountants, 1939-59.

_____. _Accounting Terminology Bulletins_, 1-4. Prepared by the Committee on Terminology. New York: American Institute of Certified Public Accountants, 1953-57.

Personal Interviews with William A. Paton, March, 1961.

THE DEVELOPMENT OF
CONTEMPORARY ACCOUNTING THOUGHT

An Arno Press Collection

Baldwin, H[arry] G[len]. **Accounting for Value As Well as Original Cost**
and Castenholz, William B. **A Solution to the Appreciation Problem.**
2 Vols. in 1. 1927/1931

Baxter, William. **Collected Papers on Accounting.** 1978

Brief, Richard P., Ed. **Selections from Encyclopaedia of Accounting, 1903.** 1978

Broaker, Frank and Richard M. Chapman. **The American Accountants'
Manual.** 1897

Canning, John B. **The Economics of Accountancy.** 1929

Chatfield, Michael, Ed. **The English View of Accountant's Duties and
Responsibilities.** 1978

Cole, William Morse. **The Fundamentals of Accounting.** 1921

Congress of Accountants. **Official Record of the Proceedings of the
Congress of Accountants.** 1904

Cronhelm, F[rederick] W[illiam]. **Double Entry by Single.** 1818

Davidson, Sidney. **The Plant Accounting Regulations of the Federal
Power Commission.** 1952

De Paula, F[rederic] R[udolf] M[ackley]. **Developments in Accounting.** 1948

Epstein, Marc Jay. **The Effect of Scientific Management on the Development
of the Standard Cost System** (Doctoral Dissertation, University of Oregon,
1973). 1978

Esquerré, Paul-Joseph. **The Applied Theory of Accounts.** 1914

Fitzgerald, A[dolf] A[lexander]. **Current Accounting Trends.** 1952

Garner, S. Paul and Marilynn Hughes, Eds. **Readings on Accounting
Development.** 1978

Haskins, Charles Waldo. **Business Education and Accountancy.** 1904

Hein, Leonard William. **The British Companies Acts and the Practice of
Accountancy 1844-1962** (Doctoral Dissertation, University of California,
Los Angeles, 1962). 1978

Hendriksen, Eldon S. **Capital Expenditures in the Steel Industry, 1900 to 1953**
(Doctoral Dissertation, University of California, Berkeley, 1956). 1978

Holmes, William, Linda H. Kistler and Louis S. Corsini. **Three Centuries of
Accounting in Massachusetts.** 1978

Horngren, Charles T. **Implications for Accountants of the Uses of Financial
Statements by Security Analysts** (Doctoral Dissertation, University of
Chicago, 1955). 1978

Horrigan, James O., Ed. **Financial Ratio Analysis—An Historical
Perspective.** 1978

Jones, [Edward Thomas]. **Jones's English System of Book-keeping.** 1796

Lamden, Charles William. **The Securities and Exchange Commission** (Doctoral
Dissertation, University of California, Berkeley, 1949). 1978

Langer, Russell Davis. **Accounting As A Variable in Mergers** (Doctoral
Dissertation, University of California, Berkeley, 1976). 1978

Lewis, J. Slater. **The Commercial Organisation of Factories.** 1896

Littleton, A[nanias] C[harles] and B[asil] S. Yamey, Eds. **Studies in the History of Accounting.** 1956

Mair, John. **Book-keeping Moderniz'd.** 1793

Mann, Helen Scott. **Charles Ezra Sprague.** 1931

Marsh, C[hristopher] C[olumbus]. **The Theory and Practice of Bank Book-keeping.** 1856

Mitchell, William. **A New and Complete System of Book-keeping by an Improved Method of Double Entry.** 1796

Montgomery, Robert H. **Fifty Years of Accountancy.** 1939

Moonitz, Maurice. **The Entity Theory of Consolidated Statements.** 1951

Moonitz, Maurice, Ed. **Three Contributions to the Development of Accounting Thought.** 1978

Murray, David. **Chapters in the History of Bookkeeping, Accountancy & Commercial Arithmetic.** 1930

Nicholson, J[erome] Lee. **Cost Accounting.** 1913

Paton, William Andrew and Russell Alger Stevenson. **Principles of Accounting.** 1918

Pixley, Francis W[illiam]. **The Profession of a Chartered Accountant and Other Lectures.** 1897

Preinreich, Gabriel A. D. **The Nature of Dividends.** 1935

Previts, Gary John, Ed. **Early 20th Century Developments in American Accounting Thought.** 1978

Ronen, Joshua and George H. Sorter. **Relevant Financial Statements.** 1978

Shenkir, William G., Ed. **Carman G. Blough: His Professional Career and Accounting Thought.** 1978

Simpson, Kemper. **Economics for the Accountant.** 1921

Sneed, Florence R. **Parallelism in Two Disciplines.** (M.A. Thesis, University of Texas, Arlington, 1974). 1978

Sorter, George H. **The Boundaries of the Accounting Universe** (Doctoral Dissertation, University of Chicago, 1963). 1978

Storey, Reed K[arl]. **Matching Revenues with Costs** (Doctoral Dissertation, University of California, Berkeley, 1958). 1978

Sweeney, Henry W[hitcomb]. **Stabilized Accounting.** 1936

Van de Linde, Gérard. **Reminiscences.** 1917

Vatter, William J[oseph]. **The Fund Theory of Accounting and Its Implications for Financial Reports.** 1947

Walker, R. G. **Consolidated Statements.** 1978

Webster, Norman E., Comp. **The American Association of Public Accountants.** 1954

Wells, M. C., Ed. **American Engineers' Contributions to Cost Accounting.** 1978

Worthington, Beresford. **Professional Accountants.** 1895

Yamey, Basil S. **Essays on the History of Accounting.** 1978

Yamey, Basil S., Ed. **The Historical Development of Accounting.** 1978

Yang, J[u] M[ei]. **Goodwill and Other Intangibles.** 1927

Zeff, Stephen Addam. **A Critical Examination of the Orientation Postulate in Accounting, with Particular Attention to its Historical Development** (Doctoral Dissertation, University of Michigan, 1961). 1978

Zeff, Stephen A., Ed. **Selected Dickinson Lectures in Accounting.** 1978